TaylorMade. Barber

"10 Ways To Do More Than Cut Hair"

Micah Taylor

Published By: Publishing Advantage Group
www.PublishingAdvantageGroup.com

Table of Contents

FOREWORD:
"TRIBUTE TO REVEREND VINCENT DIAL"

It has always been said that no one can be an island, we all need that one person or group of people that would steer us towards greatness, that would brush us up. For me, that individual is my mentor, Reverend Vincent Dial. He was my coach, and he wasn't just influential in one aspect of my life, but several.

Reverend Dial instructed bands. He was a principal and a great Pastor too. In fact, he wasn't just my mentor or coach, but also a life coach to every single person that came across his path. Reverend Dial was a very sensitive and intuitive individual. He was always aware of the littlest things around and he steered me in that direction. No matter how much I try to follow in his footsteps, his ways of doing things would always stand out. Reverend Dial would surely be missed, I do not think anyone can impact me as he did.

I have made it my journey to uphold his legacy and carry on with his life's mission. I would ensure that his principles and concepts would be adopted in the business aspect of my life. How can I do this?

One good way that I can uphold his legacy is by making sure that I carry out my obligations as a local business owner, care deeply for my customers, and also impact the lives of future entrepreneurs and people at large.

I met Reverend Dial first in grade six when I wanted to learn a band. I had two reasons for choosing to enroll in a band; one of the reasons is that it is quite rare for schools to have a band, so I had to grab hold of the opportunity when it presented itself in my school, and also, I believed it would be fun to try my hand at playing an instrument. Although the first few days or weeks were quite interesting, I was simply intrigued. However, my enthusiasm wasn't what sustained me in the band, Reverend Dial gave no room for quitting. He claimed that he saw a quality in me. I couldn't say I exactly enjoyed the band, but I had to stay because it was something that could be used to pass time as a student.

Even with my lack of enthusiasm, I was still made a section leader. I wasn't exactly talented, but then "okay" or "fairly good" is the word that can be used to describe me in the band. However, Reverend Dial made me aware of my hidden potential, he opened my mind up to opportunities I didn't even believe existed. If I think about this deeply now, the band wasn't exactly something that thrilled me. I just joined the band for the fun of it, to explore something new. In fact, Reverend Dial wasn't only my mentor because he taught me how to play instruments. No, I call him a mentor because he made me realize other potentials within me. He showed me things I didn't think possible about myself.

One of the most touching moments of my life was when I informed Reverend Diaz about this book. His response caught me off-guard because I wasn't exactly expecting it. His response moved me because he considered my achievements as also his own. In fact, this is how my good mentor has always been. He always saw other people's victory as his victory, too, even when he was the one that helped them to succeed or be elevated. Finding such people in your life or in your corner that shares your achievements and honestly believe they win when you win is truly rare and I truly respect him for that.

Reverend Dial was very disciplined, but I did not in any way consider him a "Bible-thumping minister". I would say that his legacy became one of my faiths. One of the reasons for saying so, is because he wasn't all about preaching the sermon, he was a man that cared deeply about others, and he prioritized checking up on families. In fact, my mentor loved to talk about football a great deal, he had a lot to say about the subject. This man gave me a totally different perspective of what a man of God is supposed to be like, and one sample of it is by taking an interest in not just the spiritual aspect of a person's life, but also in all other aspects.

I believe that if a person is a man of God, it should show in the character. It is not always about preaching the word of God, it is about a person's daily lifestyle. Reverend Dial made me understand that sometimes, preaching the word is not what convinces a person, but the lifestyle or attitude of the minister steering them towards God's path. I would continue to admire my good mentor for his character and how he always portrayed himself.

I really wish he was here today to see this book getting signed. I can imagine the overjoy he could have felt. I could imagine that classic Vincent smile, he would give, blessed to be at the table, blessed to be in the moment, and this is very much predictable because that was the kind of graceful attitude he portrayed. He wasn't looking for power. He didn't care for praise or attention. He was concerned about the growth of everyone around him, which I find very unique.

Reverend Dial would forever remain an incredible man, one after whom all young and older men should model their lives. Without a doubt, one for the ages. He is truly one for the ages.

DEDICATION:
"MICHAEL SANCHEZ"

Micah Taylor I can honestly say without a doubt that it is 100% an honor to have your autobiography dedicated to me. We have known each other since we were little kids and have been friends ever since. To be part of your journey means a lot because you are on a path to greatness, and nothing can stand in the way of your vision. The times we've shared on my back porch on the weekends was like a party every Saturday for the clients while you perfected your craft, and now look at where you are. You own multiple shops, educating future barbers, mentoring the youth of tomorrow and also a pillar in the community. You are someone that a kid should inspire to be like and want to follow in your footsteps to show how to be successful while maintaining your morals as a man. I'm blessed to call you my friend but even more happy to know you're family!

As a kid, I grew up in between the Carver, Keystone, and Carnegie Communities. Attended Keystone Elementary School, then Liberty Bell Middle, and finally, graduated from Science Hill High School class of 2002. During High School, I was employed by McDonald's on Browns Mill Rd, from my freshman until my senior year. After High School, I worked full-time at American Water Heaters for a year as a welder and part-time at The Buckle in the Mall at Johnson City. Fall 2003 enrolled at East Tennessee State University while working full-time at Enhanced Support Services; an in-home care provider agency. Graduating with a Bachelor in Studio Art and Graphic Design; in May 2008 from ETSU. Enrolling with the Bristol School of Hair and Design in Bristol Virginia in August of 2008. Completed the 1500 hour course testing out in Richmond Virginia with a Master Barber License in May 2010. Blessed to land a job as a licensed Master Barber at Carew Cuts Barbershop the same month as graduation. Working in downtown Kingsport Tn. In June 2010, I resigned from Enhanced Support Services to pursue barbering full time. (Extremely Grateful for the good people at Enhanced, Thank You for Everything) Worked at Carew Cuts for a total of seven years. Grateful for all the time at Carew Cuts Barber. 2016 began the renovation process to build Taylor-Made Barbershop LLC. Our original location opened in Johnson City, Tn right beside ETSU across the street from McDonald's, in May 2017. In June 2018, we constructed Taylor Made Mobile, a customized trailer turned mobile barbershop equipped with surround sound, television, wi-fi, product display case, heat & air. We branched out to ETSU student center in the spring of 2019 with an on-campus remote location, the first of its kind on a local college campus. Open for students only. In March

2019, I went back to school for my instructor's license. In fall 2019, we began construction for our second brick and mortar in Greeneville Tennessee. Also, Fall 2019, enrolled at Crown Cuts Academy as a junior barber instructor. Pressed threw the pandemic and blessed to open our second brick and mortar Taylor-Made Grooming Lounge directly across the street from Tusculum University. The support we receive from this institution is unreal. Our very first customer for the lounge was the University President, Dr. Scott Hummel. Dr. Hummel visits the shop several times per month along with coaches, professors, student athletes, and students. (Thank You Tusculum Family) In February 2020, I joined a non-profit called the Confess Project of America; founded by Lorenzo P. Lewis. Our team travels the nation training barbers/stylists in urban areas on the importance of being mental health advocates for the communities. In August 2020, I graduated from Crown Cuts Academy as their very first Master Barber Instructor to ever certify to teach. In February 2022, we completed our "Tennessee Tour" with the Confess Project, driving across the entire state educating at Academies, Salons, Barbershops, and the TN College of Applied Technology. In spring 2022, I was inducted into the Crown Cuts Academy Hall of Fame. A huge thanks to owner Craig Charles, Robin Scott, and all the other faculty and students. In fall 2022, we're awarded by the Greeneville Sun, People's Choice Award voted by the community; 2022 Best of the Best Barbershop in Greene Co. (First time ever for a Black Owned Business in Greene Co.) In September 2022, my son enrolls in Crown Cuts Academy to begin his career. So far, he has the highest test scores of any student to ever enroll. He'll be graduating soon, and to see how he's chosen to be a Master Barber on his own merit, that's the true definition of Legacy.

Jacques like myself was introduced, not pressured or forced. Like myself, as a young middle school kid, his fascination for barbering grew at an early age. Considering his natural passion for the craft and the way he handles opposition, I know without question that the brand is not only in good hands but that God strategically designed Taylor-Made to be a living testament of faith and perseverance. We've endured so much to get to this very moment, but extremely grateful for the journey. Thank You Lord for the gift of Art; by way of Barbering. This gift was truly passed down from the Father, to my father, to me, and my son. Being one of the oldest professions in the world, this craft has withstood the test of time. Barbershops are undoubtedly vital to every community. Resourceful and relatable across cultures. I consider myself fortunate to not only be a Master Barber but specifically, to be Tailor Made.

-Taylor Made Forever

INTRODUCTION

W hat prompted me to write a book in this season of my life? This is a question that has been on my mind. The answer is not far-fetched. It Is simply because I want to share my story with anyone who's ever faced adversity. In my opinion the barbering industry doesn't seem to get the respect of other professions. Although it's one of the oldest professions in the world, it is not heavily sought after as a career. From a young man's perspective, looking into coming out of high school and trying to navigate his way through life, more than likely the last thing he thinks about being is a barber. Unlike a lot of other careers, there are no guaranteed paychecks in this industry, medical/dental benefits nor a 401k. You search on Google, the average salary is $30,000 a year. So, why become a barber? In my opinion, barbering is seen by many as more of a Plan B and less of a long-term career. What's really appealing about barbering? What's fulfilling about being a barber, and more importantly are there any guarantees?

What does it lead to? What can you build on from barbering? There's no traditional form of promotion in the barbershop. If you go and get a normal 9-5 job, you can sort of climb the ladder in a lot of cases, get raises, and so on and so forth. In this industry, the individual determines the success of the chair. In other words, if you work harder you excel faster. It's all about the individuals approach to hard work. Barbering is without question a career but specifically in the area that I'm from, it wasn't very desirable at the time which I started cutting hair, back in 1998. The only barber of color in my hometown has been cutting hair for 40 plus years and he's been uprooted from his location several times. Not because of unpaid bills or any character flaws, but because the landlord inquires the space for other reasons.

Although this shop has always been a town jewel, your options are limited as a tenant. I mean for somebody like myself, picking up the clippers at 13 years old and seeing his journey, and all the unnecessary things he had to fight threw, it never really seemed worth it. Although he did everything the right way, it just seemed like at times it just wasn't enough. That can be discouraging not only on the proprietor but for spectators considering taking the same journey. Working long hard strenuous hours with retirement nowhere in sight, defiantly not something that catches the eye of a young person. In bigger cities, there are much more success stories within the industry. And that's not to say that our hometown shop isn't a success because it definitely is. In fact that was one of few examples in our neighborhood of what being a business man looked like. Coming from Johnson City, Tennessee where the minority percentage is less than ten percent, we didn't have many cultural icons to model our lives after. The popular thing to do where I'm from is to land a good job with decent benefits, and hope for the best. Clearly, barbering just seemed like something to do, and less like something that could completely potentially change my life.

My Background

I have one older sister Itiyah, but we grew up in two entirely separate homes. She and I have the same mother but different fathers. My mother and I have always had a special relationship. Despite her mental diagnosis and chemical imbalance, my mom is my heart. At her lowest points in life, she never threw in the towel on my sister and I. For that I'm extremely grateful. Considering her instabilities, I lived the earlier part of my childhood with my dad. My father is a very hard worker and is the person solely responsible for introducing me to the clipper game. As a child, I was never allowed to go downtown to the Barbershop. Kitchen cuts were the extent of my grooming. However, because of those times my fascination with cutting hair and the barbershop atmosphere continued to grow. My father was once married to my stepmother Sharon but went through a divorce my sixth-grade year of middle school. I'm also thankful for my step mom. When my mother wasn't able to be there, Sharon stepped in willingly and loved me. Nonetheless, the year of their divorce completely changed everything forever. I ended up moving into my aunt and uncle's house in the seventh grade, stayed there until my senior year of high school and back out again. From the time I was born, my environment has constantly changed. Living with my mother, father, aunts, uncles, grandparents. I'm blessed to have had family that loved me enough to step in but growing up like that, you're forced to adapt to unexpected circumstances. Little did I know, those very experiences would help shape me for the battle up ahead.

I lived as a kid back and forth from my mom to my dad's, growing up in both the Carver & Keystone Communities. So, all I saw for the most part was poverty. My father held down a full time job for many years with the airline industry working for US Airways, up until my junior year of high school. When I was born, my mother worked at the hospital as an administrative control center secretary, not long after she started having major complications with her health. Both my parents are hardworking, however I was not used to seeing black entrepreneurs and business owners. I didn't see many African American male advocates in the community. I didn't see much past either, draw a check and hope for the best or land a job and pray for job security (which doesn't exist). As a child, I also stayed with my grandmother in Virginia Beach during the summer time. I think being with my grandmother was by far some of the fondest memories of my lifetime. That's not to say that I didn't feel loved by my parents because I did, but our relationship was just so different. We could talk to each other for hours even when I was a little boy. Now that's where my faith got stirred in a different way and where I started to see life from a different prospective. There is just something special about the love and prayers of a Grandmother. Both my parents pray for me, but I'm not joking when I say, "The Neighbors Could Hear My Grandmother Praying For Me at 3am"

Mary Louise Goodman, I thank you and I miss you very much!

Family

My wife and my son are my biggest blessings. Me and my son Jacques have a special relationship. He actually has aspirations of being a master barber someday. An honor student, currently playing baseball in college. His gift is his athleticism, he is a stellar athlete. His junior year of high school, he was selected as the defensive player of the entire state for football class 4A. Winning two football state championships. Along with winning the school's first ever baseball state championship with him hitting a walk off homerun in the state tournament (Bottom of the 7th, Bases Loaded- 3Balls, 2Strikes, 1Out, down three runs.....WALKOFF-HOMERUN). He's a Legend. Although he chose to play collegiate ball, barbering is still on his to do list. I think had I never exposed him to what's "possible", he never would've even thought about being a barber. I mean, nobody in our neck of the woods thinks about barbering as a career. But because of barbering, I've afforded him a different kind of lifestyle. My wife Kara, without question is my backbone! They say that 'behind every strong man, there's an even stronger woman." That could not be any further from the truth. She motivates and inspires me in ways that I've never been before. Mainly due to the fact that we both have very similar childhood experiences. It's easier to understand someone that you can relate to. I can clearly remember my grandmother meeting my then girlfriend just one time and saying, "That's the one Micah Canelle, Don't you leave that girl! The Lord has plans for you two" Whenever my grandmother called me by my middle name I know she meant business! I now see what my granny meant. For my wife is defiantly my best friend and life partner.

We don't have a lot of money by any means, but we live life to the fullest and we enjoy each other. My wife is really the one that gave me the courage when I was in barbering school to dream bigger than I was. Specifically, she bought a Swiffer WetJet and was kind of sporadic and random. I asked her, "What's this Swiffer doing in our basement?" She replies, "That shop isn't going to clean itself silly". We got to start kind of putting stuff to the side for when you open the shop, you'll have everything to maintain and keep clean". Her just doing little things like that and speaking those words of affirmation into my life, gave me the courage to look past just maintaining a chair and clientele. Especially since I wasn't even thinking shop ownership in the beginning, not by a long shot. We've been married for almost 15 years. We have a beautiful life together. Of course, no marriage or relationship is perfect, but I do consider myself incredibly lucky.

Like myself, she kind of got the raw end of the deal growing up as a kid, broken home and not much money to go around. No outside financial assistance, had to work a full-time job in high school like myself. Had to sacrifice sports for work, like me. So, she understands me like I understand her. We relate to each other very well. We enjoy each other's company instead of just going through life together begrudgingly.

I'm currently working on getting away more and not really like lavish trips, but if nothing else, just going to the mountains and hiking. Getting away from the noise of the world. I just want to be a better father and better husband completely. Just want to make sure that when I pass away, that I'm leaving behind more than tears. I want them to be better because of my sacrifices and hard work, because they make me better. They give me a reason to grind harder. I know if I didn't have them, I wouldn't work nearly as hard as I do. I know that because prior to them, I didn't! I was kind of stagnant. Since the age of fifteen I've always had a job, but not much of a grind. Like a lot of people, I was waiting for something good to happen to me because I had been through so much opposition.

With my son, I almost feel like I've encouraged sports to help build his character. I love the aspect of team building that sports provides. You have to learn to not only play together as a unit but work through obstacles together as well. But the more I talk to him, now that he's out of high school, I'm building with him from a different level. No longer a little boy's perspective, but almost a man to man's perspective. I'm hearing a different tune. Maybe that ball was just a tool to keep him occupied and out of trouble. Maybe sports was just something to enjoy along the journey while learning character. I just want him to have an exceptional life. I really want him to get out of here, away from the north east Tennessee area completely. Tennessee is a beautiful state, so not that it's a bad place to live or anything but I'd love for him to experience different cultures and cities so that his views aren't so limited.

I just want him to be exceptional. I don't believe too much in the so called power of money, I feel like money is just a tool. But at the same time financial stress can hit really hard if not handled properly. The weight of constantly having way more bills than money can almost take you out of here. It can completely exhaust you mentally and physically. Heart attacks are real. Strokes are real. I feel like I've been borderline at that point several times, just by not having the resources or an outlet. I want my grandkids to literally be the exception of their generation. I want them to be a light in this dark world. I want the light of God to literally shine through them wherever they go and with whoever they come in contact with.

I want to retire my wife. She works hard. She's on call literally 24/7, she's in the field of in-home care services. She has a pager that goes off all hours of the night because she's one of the main Administrators. Considering her rank, if there's a fire she's got to put it out. It doesn't matter what time it is or how big the blaze, she's a one woman fire crew. She's liable to deal with something super small or ginormous at any given point in time of the day. Something basic lie a common cold or something tragic like an unexpected death. That's very stressful, although she does it gracefully. She doesn't complain but I'd like for a chance to have her at home resting.

She has an auto immune disease called Lupus and I don't want our golden years to be spent giving doctors all of our hard earned income. I want our golden years to be our best years. So I'm really, really wanting to retire her at an early age. The only way to do that is to find other streams of income outside of the chair, outside of the industry that I love so much. By doing so I hope to be able to give her a less stressful life. Rest is extremely important, and right now she doesn't rest well at all. My family is my push. My family is what I work for and the legacy that I'm trying to leave behind is for them.

Why Now?

I want people to gain hope and encouragement from this book. I'm 20+ years into barbering. I don't want to be 30 years in and doing nothing besides simply cutting hair. I would like for my career to stand for more than just a clean cut. I'd like to not just inspire folk in my industry, but also inspire someone who may not know what they want to do with their life. To encourage them in whatever they want to do, to not take no for an answer and to almost be excited by obstacles and not discouraged by them. To be able to accept life's challenges head on. You really can't win until you fail. In the environment that I grew up in, when you lose it's over. Just throw in the towel, pack up, and go home. I had to learn as I got older, losing is exciting. Losing means you're closer to the promise than you even realize. The only thing that finalizes losing is quitting. When you lose, that doesn't mean, "The End." In fact, losing is the essence to winning! Losing builds the character necessary to blaze your own trail. It's Fuel.

My wish is to spark up some hope to anyone who feels like they just can't seem to get any traction on their journey through life. I feel like African Americans as a whole, we're just so defeated as a culture. We take what we can get instead of putting in work and expecting what's rightfully ours. After all this is America, right? It wasn't until later on in life that I realized that we have been fed a bunch of crap, man. We've been told a lot of lies. I mean, even our own history has been distorted and tweaked therefore the miseducation is really what has led to our demise. I feel like now we're just feeding into the bull crap, to say the least. In the area that I grew up in, when they teach 'Black History" they ALWAYS start with Slavery. They never start from the actual Beginning. Now that I'm grown and have researched history for myself, I can see why I was so full of doubt as a child. Again, not many examples of people of color in power where I'm from. So, it's kind of hard to see a way off the hamster wheel. In my area I was fed the part of history that focuses solely on the torture and defeat. Or even worse, the murder and execution of the ones who attempted to teach us a better way of life. Dr. Martin Luther King Jr, & Malcolm X for example.

My time in college revolved around me trying to find myself and trying to discover manhood. I went to East Tennessee State University because everybody else did. I went their because I was an average student coming out of high school with no direction and my advisors and school counselors said that's the route you go when you want to be successful. A college degree, that's what opens doors. The degree is what puts you at an advantage in life. The degree will bump you up the ladder a lot faster. I went initially as a business major with the intention of landing a job at some firm or corporation in the business field. Once I got into that major I then realized how broad the business field is and that you have to be a little bit more specific and direct in order for your degree to be effective. I've always been artistic. Art was how I expressed myself as a kid. I went to a youth conference in Washington, D.C., my freshman year in college with my church and was prayed over by several evangelists and prophets.

They didn't speak barbering into my life, but they very prophetically spoke art. They just kept affirming that Art was the field in which I belonged. I was surrounded by five men and they all, simultaneously just kept saying art. Art is your path. Art is your field. You're in the wrong field. It kind of just pricked my spirit a little bit, these gentlemen didn't even know me. We had never met one another. Why is God putting art on their hearts to speak to me? Art has always been a pastime; it's not really been a passion. It's just been more or less an escape, but nonetheless I came back home and I was wired differently. I no longer saw business as my lane. So, I switched to a major in Studio Art with a minor in Computer Graphic Design and I focused more on digital media, illustrator, adobe photoshop, and all that good stuff.

As a college graduate I submitted a few resumes, but to my surprise I kept hearing the word internship, internship, internship. It didn't really scare me, but I keep hearing about non-paid internships. For somebody who paid for college out of pocket, no scholarships, no parental support, literally living off canned goods the entire time... I really got offended basically hearing, "you've just not done enough yet kid." So, come and slave for us until we say time is up and we'll let you know if you're good enough to be accepted into our corporation. I found that to be a huge disrespect, even a slap in the face. I already had my barber tools, even a few clients. Definitely not a lot of money but enough to pay a light bill or two. I graduated college May 2008 and enrolled in barbering school August 2008. I graduated from barbering school two years later, working a full-time job on a graveyard shift in order to pay for my barber tuition.

Coming out of barbering school I did not really know which way to go, I just knew I needed money, I needed a job badly. I searched the entire area and the only chair available was an hour from my house. I landed a job at Carew Cuts, a barbershop in Kingsport TN. I was fortunate to work with someone who had 30 plus years' experience in the industry and willing to mentor me. Richard Jackson, the gentleman who I worked for had the biggest ministry our area has ever seen prior to barbering. He lived life with such optimism, like nothing was as bad as it seemed. He saw what could be, not what was. I wasn't use to being around conversation like that before. Working in an environment that allowed me to grow for seven years, I finally got the nerve to branch out and open a shop of my own. So fast forward to 2016, I plant my first location in Johnson City, Tennessee. I put it directly beside the college that I went to because I know that there are several kids on that campus specifically out of state, that were a lot like myself. No parental support, no money, no direction & not much guidance.

I wanted my shop to be, more or less, a safe haven for those kids. But at the same time a pillar for my community. Since then, we've been able to really witness to a lot of college kids, man, a lot, a lot of college kids. Fast forward to 2019, we planted the second location beside Tusculum University with the same mission as the Johnson City location, just wanting a chance to reach the youth. I feel like as older men, if we don't do what we can to help them, redirect them, shape them, we're kind of doomed because they're going to be the ones in the driver's seat, leading this nation sooner than later. We can't expect them to be fully equipped, no more than we were as younger men. Young people these days are exposed to a lot of content and information, but that information in most cases is not being applied.

When we're up in age and in our golden year, so to speak, if they're not equipped to do the job I feel like they'll throw us 'old folk' off a cliff somewhere and completely disregard us because disrespect is at an all-time high. Today's youth don't hold the same regard for their elders as my generation did. I feel like when we were kids, respect was understood. It wasn't really talked about, you just knew not to disrespect someone older than you. These days respect is not talked about, it's not addressed, it's not really a thing anymore. So I feel like having a place close to campus and having those hard conversations is more or less my calling through my craft. Addressing issues in the open with no reservation. Sharing with people my challenges and hopefully adding value to peoples life while giving jobs and offering a service.

Life Crisis

The first shop I worked at in Kingsport, I spent almost eight years there building a clientele and a name for myself. Once I felt like I had topped out at that location and had invested enough time there, I made a decision to leave. I ended up going 30 minutes in the opposite direction with a third of my clientele that followed me. No manpower to help me cut, a large influx of new people coming through the door, no chair rent to supplement for the overhead and bills. Very, very, very little breaks. Maybe like two lunch breaks a week for the first six months in business. I lost a lot of weight and my health took a hit. For the record, I don't recommend that anyone go to those extremes just to get established. Know what it takes to sustain a business before you jump into business. Nonetheless, never run from life's challenges. Those very challenges may help build your foundation.

I had no idea what it took to open a business. I literally just opened. I learned taxes as I went, I learned insurance as I went. I just literally jumped and I jumped into a big, big, big mess, but as crazy as it may sound it was so exciting. I didn't see it like that. I saw it like, "I dreamed about this, I worked for this, I even prayed for this, and we're here. We're going to make the most of it". That's just what I did. I hired a few guys from the barbering academy that were set to graduate prior to our opening date. Their graduation got prolonged, which led to me working even more time by myself. It's best to go into any business with adequate manpower.

My first hire was meant to be more of a partner and less of a booth renter. Him and I had literally met for almost a year prior to the grand opening, just brainstorming and planning the business. The whole time, the gentleman was literally using me for a means of getting his barber tuition advanced. So, once he gets equipped and everything repaid nine months later, he says, "Thank you for the time and assistance, I appreciate everything you've done for me. I'm leaving to open a barbershop by myself" I learned very early in business to expect the unexpected. I also learned the importance of contracts and proper paperwork. Taking peoples word and expecting them to live up to their word is a naive way of approaching any business situation, trust me. But hey, you live and you learn. I'm just grateful to have gone thru that early on in my journey instead of later on. So, I'm down a potential partner, as well as a booth renter, manpower, experience, support, all the above. Six months later, one of my other barbers accepted a position at a Barbershop in New York. A month later, my last barber leaves to go to a shop that only takes appointments. Stating that he doesn't want to "Cut So Much", which leaves me down to one barber. For the first year and a half it just became a revolving door of barbers. No consistency, nobody comes with a plan or purpose. So, I'm just hiring people to fill chairs to help keep the line moving. I'm bringing in people instead of potential, not necessarily bad people just bad for the business. The shop in Kingsport that I worked at, in comparison to the first location I opened, cost me five times more in overhead in comparison to the booth rent that I paid. I had no clue what it took to keep a business open. When barbers are coming and going constantly, you can't really rely on that as a supplementation, their support nor their manpower. So, a lot of early mornings and late evenings to say the least. A lot of 5:00 A.M.s to 9:00 P.M.s, a lot of seven days a week, a lot of stressful days, man. Very, very taxing. Fast forward to the present day, I think we've got a little traction. I've learned that just because somebody wants a job, that doesn't mean you hire them. Companies locally like, say Eastman Chemical Company, you have to go through a pretty strenuous hiring process to get hired on at Eastman. You don't just sleeze your way into Eastman.

So, I realized early on in my journey that I'm letting people into Taylor Made way too easily. People who have not proven anything, not done anything significant, not invested anything, just literally showing up with a plan of taking what they can get. Those experiences taught me a lot of patience. So, I currently have several empty chairs. My plans are to keep it like that until I can find more personal accountability and trust with a new hire. I'm hopeful that the right people will continue to come because I am starting to see a better quality of barbers come into the locations. Not only doing well for themselves but wanting to stay and be a part of something bigger than all of us. Showing up with something to contribute. Barbering is unlike a lot of fields out there, whereas you exchange time for a paycheck. I don't give my barbers a paycheck. In fact, they pay themselves whatever they want, depending on how hard they're willing to work. That's pretty amazing if you stop and think about it because not many career fields give the employee free rain over there salary. If you need more, do more and you'll get more. It sounds pretty simple, right?

But most people, not just barbers, but people in general; run away from hard work. Nobody wants to work hard. I just find it really uncanny that there's not a lot of industries where you can pay yourself. It's almost like you're given a blank check and you fill in the amount based on your hustle. So when I see the opportunities in barbering, even personally fresh out of barber school; my mindset was "let's go", whatever it takes. Most barbers that I've encountered are just not wired like that at all. I don't know if it's because of their upbringing, their current options, or their personal challenges they've faced in life. I'm wanting to really get a grip on that, and get back to cherishing the rareness of the craft. I see a lot of folk work jobs for 40 plus years and all they get is a holiday turkey and a little small severance package, just modern day slavery, to say the least. Sacrificing everything, only to get so little in return. In barbering, the more you sacrifice, the bigger the potential return on your investment. Why would you not sacrifice?

So when I'm offering these barbers a chance of potential freedom, if you will, and they don't take it, don't want it, or kind of shun it, it's really disheartening and offensive; considering how hard I had to work and what I had to go through to get certified to cut hair. It's disrespectful to the craft as well as the industry. I know several young barbers who have retired in their early forties, early thirties even. Completely done working. They've saved and invested their money the right way. They've opened other businesses outside of the barbershop. They've invested in real estate. They've paid their homes off, their cars off, put their kids through school. I know what the industry can provide, but none of these gentlemen who have done these exceptional things have done them by just showing up to the shop, sitting on their hind parts and waiting for somebody to walk through the door for a haircut.

They're very exceptional in their outlook on life, very specific style and work ethic. So I'm really, really trying to get that part across to my barbers. I don't want you to work here for the rest of your life, but if you are going to be here, I want you to contribute something. I want you to be here with a plan, even if that is to have your own shop. Let's discuss that, let's talk about what it takes to do that while being open and honest. With that being said, to the current date I've assisted six barbers with their transition into opening their own shops after working under my brand and having come to me boldly saying, "I want my own, will you to teach me how". Hey, let's do it, I have no problem with that. My only issues are people with underlying motives and hidden agendas. People who are sneaky with their plans. I'm very open and honest with my employees. I'm not secretive about my decision making. Even if it makes them uncomfortable, I'd rather they hear about my plans from me personally versus a third party. I have no tolerance for shadiness, I don't respect that.

I think it's really unnecessary because I'm the kind of guy that wants to see everybody win. I don't want you to watch me eat, I want us to all break bread together at the same table. I mean, even if you're making more than me, I'm not offended by that. If we're all winning, if we're all up, that's beautiful harmony. I don't know too many CEOs, that share those same sentiments. In most jobs, the energy is "What can you do for me?" And "I'll tell you how far you can go". There's no love behind the mission. The modern-day workforce looks like, people plugging other people into their agenda. For the most part, we've all been pawns in someone's chess game at some point, and that's not a good feeling. I run my business completely opposite and I almost feel like for those reasons at least the first two years, I was shooting myself in the foot. Maybe brotherly love isn't the best approach to business, maybe consideration and community support doesn't work because I'm getting the wrong end of the deal.

Perhaps "Business is Business."

I'm getting shafted, I'm not getting a return on my investment. I'm just getting a bunch of lame excuses, to say the least. But learning from that, growing through that, I think it's brought us to this point. With writing this book, I just want to more or less encourage anybody with a dream. You've got to protect it. You have to be faithful to it. You've got to invest in it and more importantly, you got to believe in it because nobody else ever will. Nobody else cares about your dream, it's yours. God gave it to you for a reason. So, you have to really harvest that and protect it with everything you've got. There's nothing at all wrong with treating people with respect, but never allow people the opportunity to disrespect your investment. If you're going to be the kind of leader who gives respect, demand it in return. Never except money from people who don't have respect for the brand. There's no amount of money that's worth that sort of disrespect.

Business Growth and People Management

At the first location we have eight chairs. Opened now for six years, we offer a wide arrange of services from facials, waxing, braiding and dread locks. Not to mention any type of design work imaginable. We have six chairs in our second brick & mortar which has been open almost three years now. The third location is our newest project and is a remote studio with just two chairs on the campus of East Tennessee State University inside the D.P. Culp Student Center. Last but not least our mobile cut truck. The "Barbershop On Wheels" We consider this to be cuts with pure convenience. This unit is used for wedding parties, community outreach and numerous other necessities. Comes fully equipped with surround sound, television, product cabinet, heating and air.

I see life through one angle, which is go. I've been blessed to work with so many different types of people and I've pulled something from each of them. Instead of me managing people, they've also helped manage me. They taught me that there's other ways to look at life, that life doesn't necessarily have to be the hard way up the mountain like my story illustrates. That's just my story, that doesn't mean that's the only way to get up the mountain. I've had to learn that through working with some exceptional barbers. Even people that have literally had everything handed to them, having just as much zeal, work ethic and compassion as I do. It wasn't until I met these barbers that I learned, there are several ways to crack a walnut, so to speak. I have had some guys that have challenged me, almost on a daily basis. I think those challenges made me a better person, as well as a better supervisor.

I definitely have a better way of communicating, whereas before, I was easy to snap. I would overreact Very easily just because I was so frustrated and overwhelmed. I've been to the bottom in order to get licensed and here come these new comers literally just show up and get paid. Not much sacrifice, a lot of barbers have a false perception of what it takes to get established and keep consistent clients. Most want to cut people when they feel like, and even attempt to come in whenever is convenient for them. Being so busy when I initially opened for business, I didn't really take time to get a grip on the business. So, I had to learn to hold folk accountable while at the same time, holding myself accountable. Me leading by example and not just by command, so to speak. I can't expect a barber to be on time if I'm coming in right at 10:00, especially if we open at 10:00. If I'm the type of owner who works business hours, I should be one of, if not the first one through the door. As well as one of, if not the last one to leave if I'm the leader of the group. Some bosses lead with giving orders. In my opinion, the best bosses lead by example. If I've never experienced nor overcame common challenges within the industry, I have no business supervising people dealing with those same challenges.

I can't expect anything out of you that I'm not willing to do myself, or at least attempted myself. So even the challenging employees have made me a better supervisor/leader and have helped me to sift through a lot of people's inconsistencies. I can see malicious intent from a mile away now, whereas before, I was kind of naive and just needed help very badly. Early on I'd just take any kind of help I could get to keep the line moving and get through some of the most insane days imaginable. When you have a shop where all the barbers are filled up, and you have customers walking through the door by the fives with nowhere to seat them, that's stressful. Because you can only cut so many heads in an hour or better yet at one time.

I hate losing business. I hate turning people away, especially due to lazy barbers. I've experienced everything from barbers taking lunch break for an hour and a half, or even worse coming in two hours late because you partied too hard the night before. If we're losing business like that, that's not the Taylor Made way. I had to learn that it's okay to let them go and pull up my bootstraps a little bit, dig a little deeper and work a little harder. That's a supplement for their lack of attendance, their lack of being accountable, cutting, and contributing. I'm going to let you go willingly. I'm going to do your job and my job until I can find somebody that's willing to do your job and do it gracefully. Do it with a smile and not begrudgingly. Do it respectfully, do it professionally. Not rushing through the cut, but enjoying the process of the haircut, enjoying the conversation. Enjoying the fact that there's very few places that men have to go, to release and just be men, vent, talk, build, grow, and network. Please don't kill the vibe in the Barbershop!

Women have spas, nail parlors, salons, and other outlets. Men however, we're kind of at the short end of the stick. With that being said, lets cherish the barber shop. Don't take away the male oasis, if you will. Let's preserve that and keep it pure for what it is. Finding that balance and holding everybody accountable, but being the main one to lead the charge of accountability myself. That's been one of the biggest challenge in business thus far, not being scared to let go, and say, "You know what, you're just not Taylor Made material". Doesn't mean you can't cut or you're not going to be a good barber or have a good career, however you're just not a good fit for this establishment".

In the beginning, disconnecting was almost gut-wrenching to do because I'm losing money to help pay bills that at times seem never ending, I'm also losing manpower to help take care of customers. In the beginning I was almost nervous to fire people. Now, I fire fast, and I hire slow. I love it because I've absolutely learned my worth and I've learned that not everybody deserves a seat at my table. Not that my table's better than anybody else's, but I've handcrafted every inch of my table. If I'm buying the food and cooking the food, the least you can do is wash the dishes. It's kind of my new life motto. I could honestly care less who doesn't approve of this motto because it is the essence of TAYLORMADE.

Life Lessons

Don't put any trust in people, put trust in God. First and foremost, don't be misled or even excited by what people say or promise you. Nothing is as it seems, but as long as you have your trust and your faith in the Lord, you're good. I feel like I've been lied to a lot by a lot of folks that I looked up to and respected. So, I just don't want to carry that same dysfunction to people that come in contact with me, whether they be family, friends, foes, or customers. I want to be a person of my word. My word is my bond.

I want my brand to stand for more than a fade, more than a sharp line. I think highly of the precision of the craft itself, but the conversation is hopefully what they get more out of because hair grows back, in my case it falls out. I feel like strong conversations and words of affirmation last a lot longer than a good haircut does. So, when I retire or even when I pass away hopefully there's something left behind that I've left with people that will be long lasting. I pray it'll reach even outside of my community, outside of my area all together. Eventually helping somebody get through tough times like I had to endure along my journey. Life is hard, but tough times don't last tough people do!

In regards to the industry, I thought my purpose was to be a polished barber but I learned that my business is really my ministry. When someone's sitting in my chair for a haircut, I'm closer to them than you would be to your pastor while you're in church. I have just as much, if not more influence on my client than a pastor does from his pulpit. I'm coming down from the pulpit into the congregation. Now I'm in the fire with you. I'm mourning with you, I'm struggling with you, I'm concerned for you, I'm praying for you. I'm hopefully adding value to your day. Not just a good haircut, Even adding a spark of encouragement and inspiration. With life, I've learned that the only thing that is constant is change. I can't expect people to be in the barbershop for as many years as I did. These days for a barber to rent a booth for seven years is almost unheard of. Most barbers now days don't work through problems, they run from them. Then they adopt the phrase, "Shop Hopper". Change is inevitable.

I can't expect too much out of anybody. I've got to expect, if anything, more out of myself. I've got to hold myself every day to a higher standard. Anymore, I don't look at people for what they do or don't do right, the good the bad, or ugly; whatever the case may be. I just pull from each day's experiences and try to up the bar on myself. I'm really critical of myself. I'm hard on myself, very, very hard. I think that stems from what I've been through in life, not just in business.

In my relationship with God, I'm learning to lean more on Him and less on my abilities. Not just cutting hair, but life in general. My life is not my own. I didn't create myself. I didn't give myself the gift of art or barber, it was a gift from above. I don't wake myself up nor do I control my sleep during the late hours of the night. Even my own passion, it is not my own. My family is not my own. My business is not my own. I'm on borrowed time and I'm using borrowed property. So, I try to look at it for what it is and not for what it looks like.

CHAPTER ONE:
CLIPPERS IN MY HAND

My dad always cut my hair as a kid. He wasn't a licensed barber but still pretty savvy with the tools. As far back as I can remember he's had a full clientele. Not only that but he could break down a set of clippers, repair them if necessary and build them from scraps. Self-taught, no schooling nor training just Hustling. Going into middle school, everybody's rockin the styles, the Bobby Brown, the Gumby, the Nas parts, and the low and even cut or the box with a lean to it, that wasn't an option for me. So, I came to my pops and asked him for a certain style, I needed a style. Although my wish didn't get granted, he did see my interest in the craft and took it on himself to plant a seed. I first picked the clippers up at the age of 13, my pops bought me my very own set. I picked them up and I started kind of tinkering with my own head. It didn't look good at all. I wasn't confident enough to keep experimenting, so I stopped trying. Back then, I was way too concerned with what people would think or say......silly me! When I moved in with my cousin, I regained my confidence. I moved in with my aunt and my uncle in the last part of the sixth grade. I stayed with them until my senior year, sharing a room with my older cousin Brian who is two years older than me, When I moved in with them, he sort of challenged me.

Cutting Cousin's Hair

I had the trimmers, I had the clippers, but I wasn't really good with them, didn't really know what I was doing. I could do the basics, but my cousin gave me the push I needed. He kind of turned the pressure on. He would say, "Man, cut me up." timidly I'd reply, "Nah, I'm scared to mess you up." To my surprise, not to mention him not being afraid of a bad haircut; he replied "Well, check this out. You can cut me up or catch these hands, what do you want to do?" I'm not about to fight with my cousin, so I cut his hair and I noticed that we would be an hour into the cut and we're vibing and having some solid conversation. When I pulled the cape off of him, he was astounded. He loved it. I didn't think it looked all that great but in the town we grew up in, the only shop to get cut at were some older cats who were kind of fading out of style and he was elated to have a younger barber who's not only family but somebody that he can get cut from whenever he wanted to get fresh.

Whenever we went to football practice, I'd get pressured by our teammates. They would say things like, "Brian, man, who cut you up." He'd smile and say, "Micah chopped me up." So, word started spreading around, I started to cut our teammates and then some classmates and so on and so forth. So, from the age of thirteen all the way through middle school and high school I tried to find my groove in barbering. When I got to college, that's when it kind of really took off and I could see it for its full potential.

I can remember feeling the pressures of a young unlicensed barber with a big clientele. That's the same type of pressure you feel in a shop on peak hours, Weekends or even holiday's. It's the same feeling. The pressure is still applied. Either you perform well under the lights or you aren't really meant for this industry. So I still get those same nervous feelings if you will. The exact same feeling I got when my cousin, at the time weighing 260lbs compared to my 165lbs refusing to take no for an answer. So when he says either cut me up or you can catch these hands, I already knew what time it was. We joke about it all the time to this day. He pulled greatness out of me. He pulled confidence out of me that I didn't know was there. So I knew I had to give him something that he'd be proud of or else we'd end up scrapping over a haircut. I have so much appreciation for Brian. He's like more of a big brother than a big cousin. We've been through everything together. Everything that brothers go through.

I went from cutting him on a first attempt until he eventually started getting cuts twice a week. A normal person might get a cut once a week but normally people don't get cut twice a week. But because he lived with this "personal barber," he defiantly had the advantage. In a way, it kind of polished my craft especially considering his classmates were two years older than me. Any barber will tell you that the best way to get better is with repetition. I definitely had my fair share of practice. I'm 13, they're 15. I'm in middle school, so I'm looking up to the high school kids. So the fact that I'm cutting some defensive linemen and the starting running back it felt like, this might be the move. If nothing else, extra side money. I'm not cutting anybody my age. They don't trust me enough just yet. But when the guys my age see that I'm cutting guys two years older than us, I started to get their attention. They don't become customers but they become intrigued, like this dude is doing something. This barbering thing started to transpire and without me even trying to grow or market myself or build clients, it did its own thing.

Honestly, I didn't feel like I could be a professional barber until after I graduated college, Although I had cut hair all through middle school, high school and college and had a very good clientele in college; I thought like most folk in my family, the best option to advance was to get a degree and the degree would make the way and not to say that it couldn't or wouldn't but I shopped my degree around and I kept getting the same response, internship. Nobody said guaranteed position. I was hopeful that the degree was going to open up doors for me and I kept hearing that I had to still prove myself. My parents didn't have the money to pay for my college. So, I'm paying for college out of pocket while working a full-time job while cutting hair on the side. I made up in my mind early on that I'm done proving myself to people.

I began living with a chip on my shoulder. It kind of ticked me off, like what more do y'all want from me? So, I prayed to God, "show me the way" and it's almost as if I could hear him laughed at me, saying, I've already given you the way. I've given you access to these tools. You've been using them for 10 years now, I've done my part. It's time for you to do yours. So, literally, I graduated college in May 2008 and I enrolled in barber school in August 2008. I guess the summer of 2008 was when I threw in all the chips to at least try and see what I could do with these things, these tools.

My first pair of clippers, the Andis Master, which are chrome plated and don't get extremely warm in your hands with a lot of usage like most of the old school clippers. Most of the old school clippers, you run them for 30-plus minutes, it felt like a firecracker in your hand while you're trying to hold them. You can't complete several heads back-to-back. You've got to set them down, and let them cool off. So when I got that Master in my hand, it felt like the biggest treasure on earth. This is around the time when Cash Money Music was out with the popular song, "bling bling", so to me my clippers looked like something platinum almost. Andis Master, was the tool that took me over the top and opened me up to the concept that I've got to invest in my tools. I can't do a fire cut with a basic clipper.

No knock, but I can't get a Walmart Conair clipper and give you a celebrity style haircut, it just doesn't work like that. Whatever you do, you've got to invest in your tools. More specifically, in whatever you do you've got to invest in yourself. The only way to build momentum in anything you do is to invest time attention and money. You'll never go wrong investing into whatever respected craft you represent.

Clipper in Hand Euphoria

The feeling now is completely different from when I started or when I discovered myself. The feeling now is kind of weird because I mean everybody works a job to get compensated financially, but I could cut for free and be completely content. So, the feeling now is like what can I give somebody during the service of a haircut besides the haircut itself. A lot of barbers have different cutting techniques but when you sit in my chair, what is that experience like? I'm the barber, you're the customer, what are you getting other than the haircut? I've counseled so many people, and I feel like now I give you encouragement, I give you optimism. I give you faith. I give you triumph.

For those who grew up with me and know my story, know that I'm a no-nonsense kind of guy. Don't come at me with the challenges of life, so to speak, or the problems to the solution. Give me a couple solutions to match the problems, don't just give me all the problems. I try my best to live with optimism So, I'm going to give you more than a tight cut. I'm going to give you polish and a nugget to take with you that can help you through life. With hope that my services are more beneficial than just standard grooming.

Cutting Ties

Things I cut away were people who don't want the same things out of life that I do. Even family members, not just friends, but I thought for the longest, I had to be the "help" or the life preserver for people drowning and as I'm trying to help keep them from drowning, they're pulling me in with them. I had to learn that I can't help everybody, and I shouldn't even put myself in a position to think that I can or should. I've got to help myself first. I mean if you're on an airplane, and I fly quite a bit, they say in case of an emergency, put the oxygen mask on yourself first. Don't try to assist anybody else. Make sure you can breathe, then once you can breathe, assist your neighbor.

I recently got a word from a good friend of mine, a local business owner, he said, "The community feels like you're out of touch." I said, "What do you mean by that?" He replies, "When you get off work, you're not really social. Everybody knows you live an hour away, but you could at least come downtown and have a few drinks and just kind of chill and kick it." I understood where he was coming from, but I want to buy the club, I don't want to party in the club. I'm at a place in life where building holds a more precedence than "having a good time". I partied enough in my twenties. I think it would be foolish of me to continue partying, especially considering I now have a twenty-year-old. Being that I'm a barber, if I'm going to be able to retire, I have to be intentional about my spending and saving.

Pay me for your entertainment if that's what you want to do but considering I'm already working 10, sometimes 12 hours a day, I feel better getting my rest and being refreshed and not putting myself at risk of being at the wrong place at the wrong time and getting arrested. Those things can be detrimental to my career. Not only that, if I am that guy while getting a haircut that speaks light into your life and then you read about me in the paper, what does that say about my brand? I've learned to cut all the noise off as well as people's opinions of me. I've learned that it's not wise to take criticism from folks you wouldn't take advice from, because everybody has an opinion of you.

Apparently everybody knows you better than you know yourself but just learning to cut the noise off and be okay with not being in the cool kids club. "He's not social", that's not the truth. I'm just not giving too much of my time away to folk that aren't using their time wisely. Time is valuable. Money, you can lose money and get every dime back through time but if you lose time, you can't get time back. I can't just give you access to me like that anymore. It's not a pompous or arrogant statement, it's just that my time is valuable. And I've waisted entirely too much time on the wrong people. People who still to this day insist on wasting time. Waist yours if you wish, but I can't let you waist mine. Stop giving people permission to waste your time!

Misusing The Clipper

This is what I see the most. Again, I'm also a licensed barber instructor, so I teach at the barber academy quite a bit but what I'm seeing is people coming into this industry solely for what they can make monetarily. The average price for a haircut in the area I live in is $15-20, so, if you can do two an hour, you can make $30-40 an hour, which may sound like a lot of money but when you include taxes, insurance, when you include potential hospitalization, heck even a pandemic last year when nobody is allowed in the shop, what is that $30-40 an hour then? It's not a lot. So people want to come into this lane for what they can gain from it and not really for what they can give back.

Often times people will get educated on how to give a good cut but they are just robbing the community. This is one of the oldest trades in the world, literally. It goes back to ancient Egyptian times. This is not something that you just jump into to get "paid." I feel like every barber has a special place whether it be mentoring or just encouraging or uplifting people. People will literally pour their entire heart out to you in the process of a haircut whereas they wouldn't go to a counselor or a therapist as easily.

Recently, I met a young lady I'd never met before, just got her dead ends trimmed and in about a 30-minute span, she tells me that she's the result of a rape. She never met her father. Her mother is on drugs because of how she came into the world and was never really able to be a good mother to her. So, she entered this world through a horrific experience. I don't even know how she felt confident enough to even be that transparent. But considering she opened the door, I stepped in like you know what? You say you kind of entered this world through rape, but God wasn't caught off guard. He has a purpose for you. You aren't just sneaking into this earth. If millions of sperm entered the womb "On Your Mark, Get Set...GO", you won the race of millions. You won that race, so if you won that race, you aren't just sneaking into this earth. In fact, you willed your way in. You pressed your way into the universe. That's powerful.

And the fact that you are here in college right now pursuing your dream, most kids with that kind of emotional baggage couldn't focus long enough to get through a class or a semester or a year or even consider college. People who cheat the industry for what they can get out of it can never contribute to it. The response I got back from her was encouraging. She felt so hopeful, she even left the chair with a completely different posture. There is power in the art of barbering.

I don't have a favorite cut so far. Any haircuts, honestly make me happy. Trust me when I say Any cut. Just give me some clippers and let me cut, man. I'm good. I am however partial to design work. I'm an artist first, barber second. So here lately, I've been doing a lot of Holiday themed designs, spiderwebs, graffiti art. I love when somebody says "just put whatever in my head." That's when I go crazy. I go nuts and I just kind of start drawing abstract art in the head. So that's my forte so to speak. Any time I'm able to do a hair design, I make it my personal business to add as much detail as possible. That's my way of adding my signature to the haircut. Putting my stamp on it as the design guru. I don't cut for clout, I cut simply to continue a legacy that started over twenty years ago. In my hometown, there has never been a master barber to produce clean hair art with three-dimensional design, at least until now.

CHAPTER TWO:
ONE GUARD

O ne guard is a safety mechanism for the process of haircutting. If the guard is on the clipper, it's hard to gap the haircut or leave patches. The one guard is meant to keep everything smooth, consistent, and even. Guards keep balance and also protect the beginner from consistently making mistakes. This specific guard leaves exactly 1/8 inch of hair on the head while cutting. As you move up in guards, the barber can then determine the desired length. Being able to walk into a barbershop and say, " I'd like a 5 guard on the top and 2 guard on this sides and back" makes communicating an easy task. Guard talk puts both the client and the barber on the same page. Once the beginner advances in their training, the guard can be taken off and another method can be applied called; clippers over comb. The comb is also taught to be a guard.

Beginning Stage

My beginning was very humbling, to say the least. I put a lot of time, hours, and money into my tools and training. When I first started cutting, I didn't have access to a computer. Having internet access would have been a huge help considering barbering tutorials on YouTube. Being able to study hands-on techniques from some of the industry's top stylist is a major advantage. Not just haircutting techniques, but clipper reviews as well. These Master Barbers show you which tools are exclusive and how to maintain and repair your tools. I consider myself polished, even though I was a rookie fresh out of barber school. I wasn't a new beginner to the game by any means. Prior to enrolling for my license, I had 10-plus years under my belt, when I finally became certified and landed my first job in an actual shop, I thought everything would line up easily, considering I had a small following. While enrolled in school, I cut hair illegitimately out of an urban clothing store called Lenny's Clothing in Kingsport Tennessee. I did numbers in that store, man. I cut hair from sun up to sun down. Not only polishing my skill but networking with people outside of my hometown as well. I forced myself early on to be comfortable, being uncomfortable. Nothing worthwhile comes from comfort. Endurance is tested through times of adversity and exhaustion. I'm no exception to the industry nor in my area, I just simply did things early on that most barbers wouldn't do. I drove an hour on regular bases just to make a few dollars. Not only did Lenny's help me with my marketing, but I had also begun to expand my clientele into South West Virginia.

I mean, I cut, cut, cut, cut, one after another consistently. Once I came close to graduating, I stepped away from the clothing store to finish up my hours to get licensed. Conveniently, Lenny's was a block away from the shop where I eventually ended up working at. So when I got into the shop, the same customers who knew my style also knew my cutting technique as well as my character. But considering I was fresh out of school licensed, I still had to earn their business. They would not initially sit in my chair because the shop owner was a seasoned veteran. There's something to be said about a Master Barber. I assume my clientele felt betrayed considering I had once been at one time completely accessible to them. For about the first five months licensed, my chair felt empty. I had to earn the trust of the community once again. I'm in the shop and licensed but I'm getting that "new guy" vibe for months. It felt as if I had the plague or something. I'm no stranger to this community, but I definitely got the rookie treatment for sure. What I took from that experience is you have to earn your stripes in every avenue of life. Nothing worth having comes easy. If what you're wanting comes easily, there's a good chance that it won't be maintained or appreciated.

All over again, I had to earn my respect. While enrolled in school, I fooled myself into thinking that my license was going to be what validated me. I thought the license was going to open the floodgates and that I'd finally start to pick up traction and have a consistent flow of clientele. My experience was the exact opposite. I got humbled really quick, honestly. I made it a point to make eye contact and greet every customer who came in. Regardless if they came in for another barber or just a random walk-in. Once a customer crossed the threshold. I greeted them, respectfully, and professionally, "Hello, Mr. Reed, I've got a chair open. Richard is full right now. He's got another appointment waiting after the one in his chair. I'm open if you don't want to wait." a reply that I heard quite a bit, in the beginning, was, "Nah man, I'm good! I'm waiting for Rich." Occasionally, I'd leave the barbershop and go to local college campuses and cut hair for free. Trying to do anything to gain traction and expand my network. I didn't get licensed just to drive to work and watch television or watch other barbers cut hair all day. I thought to myself. "I'm driving from Greenville TN to Kingsport TN, a one-hour commute just to punch the clock. I drove from Greenville TN to Bristol VA, an hour and 20-minute commute for two years; just to get certified & license. I was naive to think that I had done more than enough to be in a position to have a reoccurring clientele. I learned very quickly that sometimes enough is never enough. Specifically in an industry where you're constantly being challenged. The only thing in life that is constant, is change. Nothing is forever, everything is seasonal.

I had to check myself and make sure that my energy was positive. Especially when the customer made it a point to be rude or passive. I had to remind myself to be optimistic at all times. Eventually, I got to a point where I accepted what was happening and I embraced it as a challenge. If a customer would say, "Nah, I'm good. I'll wait," I'd say, "No worries man, in case you're thirsty we have some complimentary drinks in the refrigerator. Feel free to help yourself. I'd say all that with a big smile on my face. Although the customer wasn't getting cut by me, they're still a valued customer of the barbershop. Not to mention, just because they're not sitting down today doesn't mean that they won't sit down tomorrow. So the same guy that used to get so frustrated was now offering you an ice cold beverage, on the house. "We've got the ball game on right now, is there anything you'd like to watch?" Slowly but surely, they started warming up to the hospitality. Not to mention, I wasn't going anywhere. I put in entirely too much work to quit!

Once they sat down in my chair and saw that I could cut with the best of the best, the nervousness and anxiety went away. People who use to bypass my chair eventually got in a habit of patiently waiting. The feeling is still so surreal at times. Going from the "rookie treatment" to having people wait over three hours just to sit in my chair. Not to mention, I never suggested nor encouraged people to wait on me. Both my coworkers could cut well, but cutting the hair is just half to process. Customer Service is the other 50%. I made it a point to be A1 with my customer service. Spending my personal money on customer drinks and shop necessities. At times, my co-worker's chairs would be wide open with no wait time and folk still chose to wait. For me, it got to a point that even if I knew the customer wasn't going to patronize my chair, I still wanted to make their experience exceptional. More importantly, I wanted to be an exceptional barber. I didn't want my career to be compared to the rest. At the end of my career, I wanted to say that if nothing else, I was the standard for my area and profession. I poured every ounce of sweat equity that I could into the craft because Barbering undoubtedly changed my life. Without a doubt, the beginning stages of my professional career were one the most humiliating, humbling, and uplifting experiences of my life. That particular stage of my life I've always referred to as, pressure.

Safety

I realized early on the importance of my position in this community. Although I'm not from Kingsport, I owe them my absolute best. These people could have chosen any other place to get a haircut but instead, they chose Carew Cuts Barbershop. That meant the world to me. I always felt like that shop was mine. Maybe not from an ownership perspective, but I spent more time there than at my own residence. I was at times overly devoted to a business that was not my own. To me, the love that was returned makes it all worth it. Oftentimes, folk would drop by just to conversate and have a good laugh. Very quickly, good vibes began to echo throughout the neighborhood. No other shop within the area offered a multicultural atmosphere. It was more than a place to get a good trim. We were known to be a safe haven for the community. A place of comfort and peace, even though the shop was right in the heart of the worst neighborhood in town. I'm grateful that nothing ever happened to the shop or any of us barbers. In our back parking lot, was Lee Projects. In front of us was 'Dale Street', where we witnessed everything from vandalism, gang violence, drug distribution, and even two murders. Unfortunately, both deaths were former customers of the shop. It's hard when customers become more like family and less like clients. The dynamic of barbering begins to change drastically.

These people needed so much more than a haircut. They needed a boost of confidence as well as a jolt of inspiration. So, I realized, really quickly, it's not about me. It's not about how much money I can make today. More so, how can I literally reshape what a barber looks like in this tri-cities region? How can I make Barbering Great Again? Especially from a young black male perspective, how can I reach them through my craft? How can I teach them the importance of community? To some of our customers, our spot was just a Barbershop. If you were to ask anyone from the Riverview neighborhood and Dale Street community, we were more like a black man's country club. There weren't too many places you could go in that neighborhood and be completely at peace. Our shop was open to any and every one. We definitely had a diverse group of clientele. Without question, we were known to be a judge-free zone. A minority-owned business with a clientele that was more non-minority. It's safe to say that we never had any issues, everyone respected each other. The shop stood for more than grooming. It was policed by the community. I think it's safe to say that people of that area gained hope when they saw professional businessmen who looked just like them. In an area full of dysfunction, we thrived in harmony. Ironically, the shop opened during the 2008-09 recession. God gets all the credit for that success, He sustained us then and continues to sustain us to the present day. I would like to think that we were successful because of our skill set, but the fact of the matter is the Lord used us to be a blessing to that particular community and specific people. It truly was divine destiny.

Word began to spread quickly about the vibe we had created in Kingsport. Surrounding areas became intrigued by the buzz which could be heard over in Norton Virginia, Appalachia, Big Stone Gap, and Lee County Virginia. Lee County High School became one of our main supporters. With over an hour commute, they traveled faithfully for haircuts. Still to this day, I'm astounded by not only the love but the loyalty we received from those young men. An area that's 98% Caucasian, these high schoolers commuted regularly to the city to patronize a barbershop with an all-black staff, in the heart of the ghetto. A small three-chair shop, but a vibe like no other. I don't believe that they came just for the cut, because there is a Great Clips in Lee County, Virginia. Getting a haircut there would have saved them not only time but money too. Why did they drive past those places to come to an urban barbershop? I learned early on, that some customers value time, attention, and good conversation as much as that professional touch. Those experiences awakened me to the importance of having a community shop. At the same, some customers are more moved by convenience. Completely neglecting the ambiance and character of local community establishments.

Guard Against

Once I found my groove and gained momentum, I started to feel more confident in my position. I also learned very quickly to guard my vision. My dream goes far beyond barbering. The craft is simply the vehicle that God chose to use to get me to my destination. I thought for the longest that my purpose was to produce the cleanest fade on this side of the Mississippi. I would later go on to learn that life is so much more than generating income and accumulating random goods. What kind of legacy are you leaving if everything involves you? Everyone works for what they can get, but very few people work for what they can give. The best way to kill a big dream is to tell it to a small-minded person. Not everyone is going to understand or support your mission, it's yours! It's important to guard your vision with your life and manifest it into reality. Dreams without goals are simply wishes. Never go against your dreams, guard them with all your heart. Guard them with everything in you and hold yourself accountable to a standard of excellence. Spend more time working on yourself than you do on other people. Focus all your strength and energy on becoming the best version of yourself.

I accredit a lot of my success to that shop but there was only so much that I could learn in a small town. In order to get the most out of my license, I had to travel and soak up as much knowledge as possible. In order to be the best, you need to learn from the best. One of the largest hair expos in the nation just so happens to be the Bronner Brothers International Hair Show in Atlanta Georgia. I have been to several different shows, but I get equipped with new information every time I go. It's almost like being a beginner all over again. I can remember getting off work after I've been on the clock from 7:00 a.m. to 7:00 p.m., then driving four hours to Atlanta arriving close to midnight. The following morning, I'd wake up at 7:30 a.m. in order to be in class by 8:45 a.m. Taking in a full day's worth of knowledge as well as learning about the most trending tools in the industry. I'd make a full day out of it, not leaving there until 7:00 p.m. and driving straight back to Tennessee only to then start my work week all over, if I'm willing to invest all that time and sweat equity into my craft, surely to goodness I'll reap a harvest someday. There's an old saying, "Good Things Come To Those Who Wait" although patience is defiantly required when pursuing your dreams, I'd like to take it a step further and challenge that saying, "Good Things Come To Those Who Hustle" So please, be sure and work while you're waiting.

I didn't build and maintain my clientele by being complacent. I put in a crazy amount of hours and at times, I over dedicated myself to my craft. I think it's safe to say that I was the heavy favorite in that shop, and that's not being cocky because I worked for that clientele, nothing came easy and nothing was given. I was never trained by the owner, I simply started cutting and learned from trial and error. I didn't excel in that shop because I cut better, I simply worked harder than my coworkers, I took full advantage of being 20yrs younger, I had more energy to burn. In this industry, time is way more important than money. I maximized my work day and made the most of my time. On average, I packed my lunch and took it with me so that I didn't have to leave. At any given time, a new face could walk in the door. It was then and still is important to make a good first impression on first-time customers. I wanted to give them a reason to come back. It's more important to build with the clients and form a relationship. Once the connection is made, the chances of them being frequent return guests are much higher. As a barber, I don't want my customer's money, I wanted their business. Once we've established a business relationship, everything falls into place.

Greatest Harvest

I guess my greatest harvest is seeing people liberated. I wouldn't call monetary gain a harvest because that's just a part of the job. The exchange of positive energy is hands down one of the most gratifying parts of my job. Most of my clients are more like family than customers. The haircut sometimes feels like a family reunion. Having the chance to impart hope and optimism to my guest daily is a huge perk. Seeing them sometimes walk in feeling defeated and leave out laughing and full of life, there's no better feeling. Everyone needs someone that they can confide in. Someone that they can trust and feel free of judgment. If we're being completely honest, everyone can benefit from counseling. Most people have a barber, but not everyone has a personal counselor. From my personal experience, people will completely pour their hearts out while in the chair getting their haircut. So, in essence, the barber chair is a lot like a grooming/counseling session. To only limit a barber's purpose to just haircutting, really devalues everything about the craft. A craft that is rich in mental health as much as personal self-care.

My harvest is helping folk find their way outside the matrix, helping them see their true value and believing in themselves. Here lately, I've been getting waves of people needing to vent and clear their minds. In the times in which we live, everyone seems so tense and on edge. Having a chance to talk and get things off your chest is important. Now more so than ever I see my career being more about community. A collective from the community to strengthen and develop the community. The good book says that "Iron Sharpens Iron". Working together has more potential gain than any individualized success.

Self-Care

I'm a gym rat. Working out is one of my favorite past times, it's the ultimate stress reliever for me. I put my Beats headphones on and I dial into the day's workout session. I'm social but I'm slightly introverted. On my off days, I don't like to hang around a lot of people. I like silence, peace & solitude. I've recently started to take up yoga. I'm far from a pro at it, but I love the mental escape of it all. I like to sit on my back porch and hear the wind blow and the birds chirp. I know that may sound kind of corny, but I love watching God's creation. Living in the mountains, I look forward to early morning sunrises with a misty fog that nestles right in the heart of the valley kissed by rays of sunshine. My peace and quiet time are at the dawn of a new day. Getting in touch with nature and appreciating the simplest of things. Reminding myself to be grateful for how God has remained consistent throughout my lifetime, not just my career. It's really refreshing to reflect on his faithfulness.

Me and my wife go biking and walking on a regular basis. We've got a few trails here in our hometown that have amazing views. We go to Asheville NC occasionally and literally just walked around. It's a very scenic area with great views and amazing food. I like to change scenery quite a bit. I don't like to stay in the same place too long. I like to see different people, experience different cultures. In my personal experience, routine change can be good for your mental health. We as people sometimes get stuck in a rut with a repeated routine. It's not selfish to make self-care a consistent part of your routine. Whatever that may be, find something that helps you break away from the stresses of life and focus on things that keep you grateful for the blessings in life. Life can exhaust you if you're not careful, it's important to have balance in whatever you do. I believe heavily in "The Grind", but I also believe in Rest.

In The One Guard Stage

Stay consistent. Don't be distracted by whatever is going on in either lane beside you. You'll gain traction by focusing on your goals and staying in your lane. You can't look at what other barbers are doing and think that they're passing you up. The only thing to compare yourself to is your last haircut. You've got to run your race at your own pace. Stay your course and find your stride in your own time but most importantly, don't over critique yourself. Each barber finds his or her stride at different times. If you catch criticism from clients that are not satisfied with your work, that's not a reason to quit or give up on yourself. That's not just with barbering, that's with anything you do. Polish comes with time and you have to put in time in order to prefect any professional trade. There's pride in being a professional. Knowing that the trade which you possess was not given but instead earned. When passion meets profession, there are literally no limits to how far the journey goes. Study your craft, master it: but most importantly, do whatever it takes to preserve it. Life can be a lot different when you do what you love to do versus doing what you have to do.

I can recall having breakfast one morning with one of my barbers and hearing him say, "Man, I just can't catch my stride." "People don't know me as they know you." Even when we walked into this restaurant, the waiter walks up to you and knows you and wants to talk to you about some personal stuff, not even haircut related." I had to remind him of the years spent building relationships throughout different communities and not just my own. The waiter at the restaurant was just one of many people that I had made it a point to connect with over the years in the barbershop. In everything I do, I try to promote the business as well as the purpose of the brand. If I go out anywhere, I make sure that I have business cards or flyers handy. Asking simple questions like, "Hey my man, by chance, do you have a personal barber?" I like to specify "personal barber" simply because most people go anywhere that's convenient when they need a haircut. I want to be the guy you keep a rotating schedule with for all grooming purposes. Someone who is not only familiar with your particular style but also flexible with schedules. I get asked all the time by younger barbers, "How can I connect with the community as you have?" I'm always mindful of how I respond to that question because most barbers have no desire to connect with the community; they're just in search of a dollar. Trying to figure out how to make barbering work in their favor. It's easy to see who's in it for the sake of the community and who's in it for a paycheck. There are barbers who work hard to build a consistent clientele, and then, there are barbers who sit in their chairs for an entire shift looking at senseless content on social media waiting patiently for a walk-in. The problem with that is, sometimes no one walks in! In order to sustain income, scheduled appointments are a guarantee.

In this game, if you don't cut, you don't eat! It's vital to the success of every barber to make the best use of time. If you're going to be on social media, at least post something for your followers to view. Don't just scroll through for hours at a time looking at things that are not going to help add to your network or your pocket. Social media is a powerful tool if used correctly. In the same regard, it can be the very tool that leads to your own demise. Abuse of this tool can be detrimental. A lot of barbers like myself have built an established full clientele without the advantages of computers and social media. Although the computer way of marketing and promoting is a great way, contrary to popular belief, it is not the only way. The old fashion way of face to face communication and contact exchange is still highly effective. The important thing is to not grow complacent along the way. Get out of your comfort zone and shake hands with a complete stranger. After you have their attention, give them a reason to tell everyone they know about you and your services.

Relating At Work

In my personal experience, building with co-workers and fellow barbers can be challenging, depending on the group. Not everyone is into team building. Some barbers have a "Me, Myself, and I" type of mentality. It's important to learn them as a person first and less as a barber. Learning what makes them tick, as well as learning what ticks them off. Also tapping into whatever goals they may be currently working towards. During my interview process with new hires, I don't start out with the expectations of TaylorMade. Instead, I start by proposing a series of questions. For example, "What do you want out of your license?" Do you currently have a five-year plan? What are some things I can help you accomplish to achieve those goals? How can TaylorMade help you in the next phase of your career?" After I've had a chance to understand their objective, I then hit them with my own. Now that we've had a chance to talk, these are some things that I expect from you. I have a standard for the shop and I expect you to help maintain that standard. If I'm willing to help you achieve your goals, I expect that same energy in return. I'm not going to continuously ask for your help, especially if I'm completely open to helping everyone on the team. Teamwork makes the dream work as long as everyone on the team is working together. Everyone must be on one accord in order to fulfill the overall standard of the business.

I think it's safe to say that I learned the hard way what not to do when hiring and firing. Before, I would start out the interview process with the latter by focusing on rules, regulations, and expectations first. Although these things are very important and vital in business, it's just as important to work toward understanding exactly who you're hiring. It literally took five years to get a nice groove and by groove, I mean great energy. We've got a serious team now. My current staff is extremely close. To the point that they eat breakfast before work occasionally, spend a full work day together and then they'll go out and get some wings and beer after work. They love to be around each other, man. It only took five years to create that kind of energy. Whereas, before, it seemed as though considering I'm the boss, certain individuals were somewhat timid to come to me about certain things or confide in me or talk to me about issues in the shop.

A recent issue I had in one of the locations was profanity. I had a customer tell me that his son complained to him that he overheard a lot of bad language during his haircut. I can honestly say that I hardly ever get a negative report about my team. They're a solid group of individuals, so instead of simply letting everyone go for hurting the overall integrity of the business, I created a "cuss cup". "Hey, guys, we've recently had an angry parent complain about profanity around small children, so since you all are having trouble monitoring your conversation, there will be a charge of $20 for a cuss word. I want to see just how important it is for you to swear when you're communicating with each other. By the way, if they talk negatively in public about our shop, they won't mention you the barber.....they'll say TaylorMade!" Addressing things like that are easy, because I don't ask for cooperation. They have a choice to either comply or move on. Considering I'm asking for something that can help the shop grow and maintain its standard, very rarely do I have a barber refuse to comply. Although it does happen, unfortunately, some people will forever work against progress of any kind. That's just a personal character flaw. Pay them no mind, remember stay focused.

Over the years, I've put entirely too much money into the brand to let an inconsiderate, selfish barber into my operation. Someone with no intention of helping the brand grow. I have no use for someone just "looking for a job". It's usually those same people who give you the hardest time, simply because they have no idea what they want out of life. Ironically, they expect you the business owner to be their plan. My barbers have heard me say this many times before, "there are three types of people in this world;

1. People who make it happen

2. People who watch it happen

3. People who don't know what is happening

It's very important that you figure out who you are early on in life. If not, you stand a huge chance of getting trapped in life's Matrix. You don't want to get to the end of your life and have a ton of regret. Nothing is worse than wasted potential. Someone who has God-given ability but does not have a natural work ethic to match that ability. God gives us gifts, but he doesn't do the work for us. He's literally given us every tool possible to live life at the highest level. Accountability is key when pursuing your destiny. More importantly, personal accountability. Taking a self-inventory and owning up to every mistake made along the way. Making a mistake doesn't mean that you've failed. You only fail when you throw in the towel and quit. Embrace life challenges and use them as fuel instead of a reason to forfeit your potential future self. Make sacrifices today that your future self will thank you for. If not, you'll be making decisions that your future self will hate you for. Everyone has the power of free will, choose wisely.

In my journey, what sticks out to me the most is that nothing is forever. The only thing constant in life is change. Everything is seasonal, nothing last forever. I've had many great barbers on my staff over the years. People who have been a true blessing to TaylorMade. Plenty of good times to remember. I like to focus on the good and grow from the bad. There is good and bad in any and every situation in life. It's all about perspective. I choose to see good in every situation. Even if it doesn't look or feel good, you can always grow in areas where there is pressure. Look at farming, when planting seeds you first have to work the ground. But in order to get growth out of your seed, you have to use strong fertilizer. In other words, during the growing process, you've got to push past a lot of S#! %

I've learned that my strong suits are haircutting. I've mastered my craft. I don't have to work at barbering, but I do have to work constantly on my leadership. I've had to learn how to properly lead. Not everyone is meant to lead, but those that are to lead should make a conscious effort to work on themselves as well as things to help the overall well-being of the group. A good leader doesn't lead by command, they lead by example. People will respect what they can relate to. If they see that you're willing to do or at least have already done what you asking of them, they'll be much more susceptible to compliance. If I'm having a bad day, I've got to learn how to tune off whatever is going on and lead with an open mind. I can't bring whatever baggage I may have going on into my work life, coming in with an attitude because I'm the thermostat. So if I'm hot, now the whole room is burning up and they feel that energy like crazy. At the same time, being the thermostat, if I'm regulated; now the entire environment is comfortable. As the leader, I can't act as a thermometer. It's dangerous for any leader to allow circumstance to fluctuate their energy. It's the job of the thermostat to set a comfortable consistent temperature. Be the Thermostat, not the Thermometer!

I don't want to be the guy that walks into a room and runs everyone out due to bad vibes. Communication can be crucial in business but sometimes actions speak a lot louder than words do. Bad body language and tone of voice can both be key indicators of built-up tension or stress. Sometimes you can say absolutely nothing and say a whole lot. Both good and bad energy is contagious. It's important to make sure your energy is proper before going into the workday. Life has a way of throwing curve balls at you. If you're not careful, life will throw you for a loop and completely distort your plans and objectives. Stay optimistic and don't let life's challenges get the best of you.

People can misunderstand your intentions based on your energy levels. If I'm completely overwhelmed, I should probably wait until I'm calm to communicate. Try your best to keep your composure when dealing with life's stresses. Control your body language as well as your tone of voice. If you're loud when trying to relate to someone, more than likely they're just hearing noise instead of whatever message you intended to convey. Composure is crucial in leadership, but for some people, it's the hardest thing to overcome. Some people know exactly what to say and do in order to get a reaction out of you. Especially a negative one. Again, the thermostat controls the environment. So once you give control over to the ones you're supposed to be supervising, it's almost a lost cause. Leaders must lead.

I recently hired a guy and before I got into the whole spiel, I asked, "If there are eight barbershops in a two-mile radius, why did you choose TaylorMade?" His response impressed me, "Well, I went to barber school with three guys that you've hired, two in your Greeneville location, one here in Johnson City, and the one here in Johnson City told me that he started his own product line and you were the first person to promote it. He didn't even have time to put it on the internet, you had put it on first and encouraged people to come shop with him. You're not insulted by his growth nor are you afraid of him promoting himself inside your business the way that you have. You actually encourage it and you know that he's going to eventually leave you one day and you're okay with that."

I was astounded by his remarks because I could tell that he wasn't just making conversation, "Well, on that note I asked, what's your plans?" He replied, "Well, my dad wanted me to open a shop in Irwin, Tennessee, but I feel like I'm not ready so I want to at least work for you for a few years." When I heard that, I was blown away, "I've never heard anything like that. You mean to tell me your pops has the money and the contractors to put you a business together right now but you're humble enough to admit you're fresh out of school, you're not ready, so you want to train under me to get ready?" I've not heard anything close to that in a long time. I hear a lot of arrogance, a lot of overconfidence, a lot of fake crap but not enough real. After the interview was over, I remember thinking to myself, we're getting somewhere now, man. Word is spreading throughout the community of the blessings of TaylorMade and people are coming to add to those blessings as well as get equipped to be a blessing.

People are getting the message. They're getting the whole purpose of the TaylorMade brand, which is not just haircutting and making money, it's everybody growing together... Everybody eating and basking in all the spoils of being in a productive establishment. Everybody elevates together in unity. My outlook on business is, if you outgrow me; I'm going to be at the finish line applauding you. I'm going to throw confetti on you when you cross the line. I'm going to be your biggest cheerleader. I'm not going to be mad at you or resent you because, at the end of the day, you're an extension of me. You can only tell a real tree if it's bearing real fruit. If my apples are rotten, I'm not much of a tree. Especially not a resourceful one. But when my apples are ripe and full of nutritious value, the entire tree grows expeditiously. So, when they tell their story, the real ones mention TaylorMade as a springboard into their own lane of entrepreneurship. More than a place to work, more of a place to grow.

Hearing that young man pour his heart out like that, I felt the enthusiasm was genuine. Even after the interview, he messages me saying, "Mr. Taylor, I want to thank you for your time. The conversation was liberating. I feel like this is the best choice for me, the best option I could've found for myself as a young barber coming out of school. I look forward to working for you. I promise you I won't let you down." I thought to myself, dude, the interview is over. Why is he still trying to convince me? Now that we've been working together for a few months, I see that he wasn't trying to convince me but instead reassure me that he is indeed a man of his word. A man of character which is rare sadly enough. In the times that we live in, being a man or woman of your word is close to extinction level. Not only does this fuel me, but it helps me to see that my past efforts are not in vain. Even those who rejected what I have to offer, I'm making a serious impact in the lives of many. People are literally being changed by the efforts of TaylorMade. Try not to force s square peg into a round whole. Whoever is meant to be in your corner, will not only be there but they'll be more of an asset and less of a liability. Stop wasting time on people who waste time. Let them have ample time to waste their own lives but don't give them permission to waste yours. Being resourceful to people doesn't mean being blind to malicious behavior. No your worth and the value of your good fortune. Know the blessings attached to you from the prayers of your ancestors. Blessings that have flowed continuously from generation to generation. Time is of the essence and is not meant to be wasted. So please, be cautious when allowing people into your inner circle. Retain a great attitude and remain a person of character, especially when others don't share those same sentiments. Be the exception to the rule, regardless of how your life started. Make sure it ends on a different set of terms. Be faithful to the process of growing and learning, but most importantly, Guard Your Dream!

CHAPTER THREE:
SANITATION "KEEPING IT CLEAN"

It's obviously good sanitation practice to keep your tools clean but what's equally important is keeping a clean heart and open mind. In my opinion, there is no need to have squeaky clean hands with a dirty attitude or nasty disposition. Can you imagine going out to eat and the waiter comes out with a beautiful display but serves it to you with a bad attitude? Or even worse, the chef prepares everything on your plate using unsanitary utensils. It's not enough to just focus on a clean restaurant. When serving the public, the entire package should be presentable. In business, small details are very important.

It's not good to go into the work day holding grudges against people or carrying any type of bad energy. Regardless of the pressure, you may be under when on the clock your job is to serve people. If you're bogged down, or your mind is cluttered, you might be able to give a good haircut but in actuality, you're not giving a good service. Believe it or not, a client can feel the energy that you have behind the barber chair. If your attention is split or scattered, you're not giving the client your undivided attention. Having broken attention robs the client, and deprives them of a certain level of customer service. From personal experience that's one of my battles. Maintaining my concentration and focus is something I have to always be mindful of. In other words, I have to war with myself to keep my heart, mind, and spirit clean, so that I perform at the highest level. If I'm not intentional in being aware of my own energy, I'm setting myself up for disaster. Instead of me handling my day, my day ends up handling me. It's important to have balance. With that said, harboring things in your heart for any reason can potentially ruin everything you've built. As you're reading this chapter, repeat this out loud to yourself; "Beware of Heart Attacks." When I say heart attacks I'm not just referring to the physical ones but the spiritual, emotional, and mental ones too.

My past experiences have taught me that when it's time to cut, I have to make sure that I go into the barbershop with a clear focus. Whatever's going on doesn't need to take precedence over my entire day. Regardless of how big or small the situation, it's got to take a backseat before I hit the door, I block it out for the time being so I can give my barbers, and my customers the best version instead of the unfocused weighed-down version. "Keeping it clean" also speaks to the focus on utensil cleanliness. Proper sanitation prevents the possibility of skin infection. Certain infections can be transferred to other clients. Depending on the severity of the situation, medical treatment may need to be applied. By law, all shops have to have a UV sterilizer before we can be cleared to open for business.

The truth of the matter is, not all barbers use this equipment. Although barbericide and clipper disinfectant should be used regularly, another good sanitation method would be to break the tools down completely. By doing this, everything gets fully exposed. All the dead skin, debris, loose hair, and dirt can be easily removed. Letting the clipper blades sit under the UV light for at least an hour kills any potential virus that could grow. It's not safe to leave room for bacteria to overtake your implements. Proper sanitation is not only a legal requirement, it also shows responsibility and maturity. Barbers should be mindful to keep the public's health a top priority. It doesn't take much time and effort to ensure, that the well-being of the people being served.

The same type of cleansing is what needs to take place in our hearts. My friend, it is imperative to take time to allow the things that clog our souls to be broken down and sanitized by positive thoughts, appreciation, and forgiveness. Taking time to deep clean our hearts and clear our conscious should be an equal part of our cleaning routine. I call this method, "Internal Sanitation". Focusing all your energy on the things that need to be removed from your life. At times, that can even mean other people. Putting distance between yourself and people who don't add value to your life. A person should never continually pour from an empty cup. Never apologize for being intentional about keeping your personal space productive & positive. An extra emphasis on being Positive. There is way more than enough negative energy in this world.

I've discovered that it's the small things we neglect that manifest into larger things we can't ignore. We often try to cover up our heart wombs with superficial Band-Aids of denial or avoidance all the while engaging in our next set of relationships.

During my time as a licensed barber, I've witnessed entirely too many barbers who don't spray their tools down with disinfectant, cleaners, or use UV sterilizers. They just cut, cut, cut, cut, cut without cleaning their tools. When their blades clog up, they just buy new clippers as if that's the solution to the problem. Completely masking the problem instead of addressing the problem. An older blade is a better blade. You don't need new blades. You need to take the blades you have and break them down, treat them right, love on them a little bit, and you'll get the best version of what that tool can possibly provide.

What if I told you that you may not need a new spouse, friend, family, job, home, or car? What if I suggested the benefits of a heart change, which could make the overall difference? Learning to preserve the things you already have. In most cases, we don't need replacements but instead just a simple realignment. I've learned this through trials and many errors but when I grasp these concepts and applied them daily, my life has never been the same.

Barbers should sanitize all of their equipment not just their specific tools, but capes and chairs as well. For example, when you're cutting kids specifically; if you give them a sucker most likely drool runs all down their mouths and all over the cape. I've seen barbers that'll use a cape for a solid year and once it gets a rip, they'll throw it away. It doesn't require much effort to take that thing to the laundry or to the dry cleaners and drop it off. They'll literally have your equipment right in no time. Failure to clean properly is sloppy and lazy to not sanitize, and disinfect all your equipment. Believe me, I know that the barbershop is a busy place and time is valuable, but a clean shop is a healthy shop.

Now with COVID coming on the scene and the focus being heightened on sanitation, I see barbers using disinfectant sprays to spray the chairs down, but that should have been a daily practice prior to COVID. Consider fall season, flu season, everybody's sniffling and snorting, stuff's in the air that you can't see. Remember, just because you can't see it doesn't negate the fact that it's there. Whatever they touch, sit on, or come in contact with is potentially infected. Routine cleaning should be a must in between every haircut. Take at least 10 minutes between a service, sanitize your chair, at least spray off and brush off your tools. Spray at least your cape, and give that stuff time to dry and set in before you bring in the next client instead of just running them through like a mill. The door handle of the shop, bleach wipes, wiping them down.

The remote controls also need to be cleaned. Sounds crazy, but barbers are constantly changing channels. Don't just put your tools up and cut the lights off and walk out. Really go through the place and mop, vacuum, scrub etc. like grandma used to do. She had nothing left unturned. Grandmamma cleaned everything from the top to bottom. Having that same mindset as our grandmothers had, just thoroughly deep cleaning, I think that should be implemented in the shop to be a good barber. It's not just about a good haircut, but how deep you can go with your sanitation, and your cleanliness.

It is not just the shape-up and fades, it's about the entire experience and environment. Note this, my heartbeat and motive behind the chair need to sound louder than my trimmers ever should. The services are void and mute if I don't keep my heart clean in my shop.

Sanitation

In the first shop I worked in, I cleaned it religiously. I got so tired of hauling trash in my car down the block to a random dumpster, that I eventually paid for waste management to have a place to dump our trash. I bought trash bags and cleaning supplies regularly. I cleaned the entire place, the toilet, the counters, indexed the mirrors, mopped, and swept. Not that this was asked of me, but I saw that most of the time if I didn't do it things go overlooked. I got sick and tired of turning the key to open the store and getting knocked down by the smell of trash bags piled up in the back. I had a great relationship with the owner, but eventually, I came to my senses and said to myself, "If I'm going to be putting this much effort into cleaning, opening & closing a business... It should be my own!" That shop had so much potential man. We definitely had some great times, but everything in life happens in seasons. My time there had come to an end.

Even as a kid, my barber in Virginia had a fifth of Hennessy on the station, he was half drunk most of the time I sat in his chair. He'd give you a decent haircut, when that bottle gets low, your line is going to be slanted in whatever direction his hand would drift. To add insult, his tools wouldn't be clean at all. I've seen rust accumulate on the blade of a barber's tools. That can kill a client. I never really thought much of it as a kid, it was honestly the norm, as I grew and started studying the trade of a Master Barber, and I'm horrified by my childhood barbershop experiences. Complete neglect would best describe those visits.

As I was doing my own research, I found that microscopically, up to 10 to 20 germs, however you want to quote it, can fit on the tooth of a blade. So if you were to count straight across, it's almost like 100 microorganisms that can take you up out of this world in the hands of a barber's clipper. Safety matters and should not be something that's experimented with. Razor blades are mainly disposable blades now because back in the day they used the strap and the hone when they sharpened the same blade in between every cut. When AIDS came on the scene in the seventies, and eighties, the industry implemented the use of disposable blades.

Even now, with the use of disposable blades, I see a lot of guys just keep the same blade in the shaft simply because it's convenient. Grabbing the blade and dragging DNA from one client to another client. I'm a businessman and really it sickens me because it doesn't take much time to keep people safe. It really doesn't and seconds can save both a life and a lawsuit. Sadly to say, most barbers focus more on money because time is money and I get that, but you're going to spend more money losing people and potentially getting sued over malpractice & over not taking care of your stuff. I'm ashamed to say I've seen that more than I've seen proper sanitation.

One of the reasons I wrote this book is to educate the masses who never will see the barbershop from my view or perspective. Sanitation is a requirement, not an option. I strongly enforce these practices throughout the shops I own. In the past and present, we have had regular meetings to discuss the cleanliness of our shop. We just had a meeting recently where I went over the good, the bad, and the ugly. I praise my staff for the good and I even reward them for the good. I've even discounted booth rent to positively reinforce the standard and even celebrate excellence. On the other hand, if you are not up to code you get one verbal warning, and after that, you're terminated. Unsanitary behaviors can't be tolerated in my shops. Dr. Mike Murdock said something profound. "What you tolerate you cannot change." Again, I don't think cleanness is something that needs to be gone over again and again. If I let staff slack on sanitation, they're literally holding my shop's name hostage and just running it through the mud. So now, the standard is compromised from their lack of attention to detail. That's just not acceptable because they're not going to say "Ray who works at TaylorMade messed me up". They're going to say TaylorMade, they jacked me up. Don't go to them. They're not clean. They're not right. My name and brand are on the line, not my staff's name. You can leave my shop and go get another job and you're good, but my reputation is still compromised and that's not fair. So, if that's too much to ask, I'd rather you go waste somebody else's time. Truth be told, if you can't uphold that, I'll find somebody else that can.

Cleaning Your Heart

Maintaining a clean heart is a key factor that I live by and enclosed inside this chapter. Repeat after me "my heart is everything." I didn't realize how important protecting your heart was, especially in my rookie years so to speak, I was fresh out of school. To be honest and keep it 100 with no chaser, I had a very rough childhood. My upbringing was turbulent and my family background is pretty dark. Throughout the course of my life, I held a lot of the pain I had deep down on the inside like a vault buried in the sands of nowhere. Often, I simply went numb and blocked out all the pain in my heart as a defense mechanism. What I didn't realize was what you push down will come up to the surface with greater force or velocity back to the surface.

As a young barber, I would open up and go into my family issues all because I was hemorrhaging emotionally. After becoming older and more seasoned I later realized that it's my client's turn to share. My client didn't pay for me to transfer my issues and emotions onto them, they came to get their haircut and then leave. Quickly, I learned to tuck that away and have an open ear for what my customer has going on. In this case, if there is something going on with me, I need to seek counseling for my issues, and what I've been doing in the past seven years is getting up two or three hours before 10 o'clock meditating, and working out. These are my best times and the highlight of my day. Whatever I got to do to clear my conscience to make sure when I go in the shop I'm ready to go and that I'm firing on all cylinders. Whatever comes my way potentially that day can't block the mission because I've equipped myself and gotten up with enough time to be able to fight this battle. I am getting a jumpstart to my day, where a lot of guys literally wake up and the alarm clock goes off, smack it to get that extra five minutes, 10 minutes of snooze. Not me, I'm up to get my spiritual download before I take on the workload.

My counterparts are rolling in the shop with crust in their eyes, they aren't even halfway awake with a bag of Chick-fil-A mini biscuits that still have to be consumed before they start cutting. It may sound funny but it's true. Word to the wise, if you are arguing with your baby mama or something going on with your kids, of course, you're bogged down. You're not giving yourself time to get acclimated. So having a clean heart, an open and clean mind, is just as if not more important than having your physical heart checked. Clean hands and a pure heart are just as important as the cleanliness of the tools and the shop.

CHAPTER FOUR:
THE FADE

In my opinion, if you can't fade you can't cut. Blending everything together is one of the most sought-after skills or techniques that a barber can have. You can tell a barber's skillset if you can't see any lines in his fade. Nowadays, they call this the "blurry fade". If your fade is blurry, which means it doesn't even look like it's real, you knocked it out of the park. The fade game has many different techniques. The goal is to elevate the lines and produce a natural-looking blend for the client. Personally, I quit using guards over 10 years ago, because to me, it takes so much time away from the process. I want to make a point here to stress that it is imperative to find out what works for you and discover what techniques give you an advantage. Clippers in my hand are not the same in the hands of another barber although they may be the same brand. Yeah, I know you may be saying what is Micah talking about. Please let me clarify. Although two barbers may be using the same set of clippers or tools, their techniques will always be different. Each barber will bring their own originality or style to the cutting process, as they both learn what works for them. Never stop learning and bringing your true self to your profession no matter what it is, be faithful to yourself. The more I learn, the more I unlearn and evolve.

In the beginning stages, you start with a zero, then you open your lever to a half, then you go to the one. Then you put a one and a half and the two and so on and so forth. So, there are literally steps. You literally make a line, fade out a line, make a new line, fade out a new line. The back and forth may seem redundant but through the faithful process of repeating the steps, one perfects their craft and the art of fading. My friend, I encourage you to do things on repeat no matter how it may feel and how senseless it may seem, it will perfect your outcome.

Using my technique now I literally fade in one stroke. So, with my comb, I swipe, cut the desired hair and comb it away. Meanwhile, I'm fading, each stroke is a fade. Remember when I said early on, that doing things on repeat perfects your skills, I wasn't lying. Now, I have coworkers that look at me, they'll sit and watch me cut like, man, how do you do that? It just comes with time and repetition I say. Trust me, if you do what you are called to do over and over again, it will become like second nature to you and people will marvel at the end result of your faithfulness to your craft. Be mindful, people will always try and emulate your end result, but neglect the process that it took to get you to the end. The process is very necessary, so learn to trust the process. It builds character.

It's a really unique technique because very few barbers can do it, but not only does this save time, but it's also soothing. It's a skill set that not many have learned to master. Hear me when I say this sincerely, I'm not the greatest barber of all time, but I have invested a lot of time, blood, sweat equity, and tears into striving to offer the best service possible. I feel like in your career as a barber, at every level you go, you fade away from certain things and sometimes even certain people. Sometimes in life, you cross the line and you have to cut it out. In other periods in your life, people cross certain boundaries or lines and you have to sever those lines. You fade away from certain mindsets. I can't tell you how many times I've had to change my mind for the better and step away from stinking thinking. You fade away from complacency, from people who just conform to whatever life throws at them. Oftentimes, I personally had to completely fade out or disappear from environments that were not conducive to growth. This wasn't easy and it left me in some vulnerable spots but it preserved my peace and kept me on track for the greater vision. Never be afraid to lighten your own load or die away from the people, places, or things that attempt to kill your dream(s).

The higher up you go with your technique, the more you invest in extended education and the more money you put into your tools will oftentimes make you a target in the barbershop. Simply because the industry is filled with complacency. This is mind-blowing because the secret to this industry is quite simple if you want more; do more. It's foolish to think you can show up to the barbershop (at your convenience) and still reap the benefits of hard work. Hard work works, period! No one has ever invented a substitution for hard work. For whatever reason, people will often times play the blame game instead of simply accepting responsibility for their own lack of effort. They'll blame you for their shortcomings, although they have access to the same information and resources as you do. Even though you're in the same shop and targeting the same group of people there is just something different about you. You and your counterparts have the potential of cutting the same clientele, but you've elevated and they haven't. Is that your fault? I'll answer that question for you. No, not at all.

People who refuse to pour into their own success tank do not take a self-inventory of what they're not doing. As a direct result, they lack professional development, their fade techniques are not as clean. Or they're rushing through the hair-cutting process and when somebody gets out the door, and the sunlight hits their head, you see all sorts of fade lines. As barbers, if we aren't careful, we can find ourselves just rushing the cut, trying to get to the next customer, attempting to get the next dollar. In essence, that type of barbering is detrimental to the overall morale of the shop, as well as takes away from the overall respect for the craft. Good things take time, that's with any industry. Customers who appreciate quality will respect the process. To be quite honest, for those customers who don't respect the process and time, you don't need them on your appointment book. As I mentioned before, all money is not good money. You want people who bring good energy to your establishment. All energy is contagious, both good and bad. So it's only wise to create an atmosphere that is conducive to good vibes only. Respectfully, but also unapologetically.

Properly fading takes time and takes practice. Fading or blending demands attention to detail. The same is true for people when you fade away, you don't look back, you cut that weight. You accept it for what it is because, on the journey to success and greatness, everybody can't go. Freeloaders don't deserve a ticket on your bus. Everybody is awarded the chance. I believe that wholeheartedly. In my opinion, I don't think anyone is exempt. As for me, I don't believe in extraordinary people. I believe in incomparable focus and unmatched hustle. If you can muster up enough strength to just tap into that, anybody can get their ticket punched in my opinion, but it's odd that a lot of folks don't. That's a personal choice I believe. Many refuse to seize the moment or to hone in on the greatness within.

Getting up early and mapping out what today needs to produce in order to get to the next level. Doing the above causes you to focus and fade out the grey areas. Like when I came out of barber school, one of my mentors and life coaches made me write out a five-year plan and keep it in my wallet, and called me randomly to ask if I was on track. He would call me and say "Okay, are you hitting the quota for this week to make sure this is a successful year one?" After year one, he stopped calling me because he knew I wasn't going to let him down. I'm not that great, he just saw greatness within. The same greatness that's in us all, if we only choose to tap in. Note, I realized that I had a shot and decided I wouldn't play around with it. You, reading this book at this very second, I believe you've got a shot no matter where you've been and what has happened in your life. If you learn how to fade and blend, you will make the cut. Knowing when to fade to bald versus when to blend in makes for a perfect combination to bringing your goals or dreams into manifestation. The first thing that I would recommend to anyone who's determined to excel, is being intentional. Ask yourself the hard question. What are my intentions for my life or business? Being calculated with your game plan, intentional with your efforts. Not just waking up and hoping it's a good day, hoping the shops busy. Hoping or wishing you learn a technique but rather plan to be in a learning environment. Being intentional, being prompt, being exact, and being purposeful is all a part of becoming deliberate.

Recently, I was cutting a long-time client, a gentleman that has literally been in my chair since I was 17 years old with a mutual friend of ours also in the room. The client had asked what my next move was, I mentioned a desire to sell art. Previously, my wife had hired a photographer to take an aerial picture of my new location in Greenville from the campus zooming in on the location. I made a comment that I want to start selling custom-made art, TaylorMade art. To my surprise, the gentlemen didn't expect a sincere response. He asked the question insinuating that I had already accumulated enough.

Out of nowhere, the client says, "Bro, you're getting greedy." I was completely astounded, especially considering I was asked this question and wasn't volunteering the information. "What do you mean?" I asked. He replies, "Man, you've already got multiple businesses, what else do you want?" I replied passionately, 'Man I want it all bro!" I want everything that I'm willing to work for. There's an inheritance with my name on it, and I want everything that God has for me. I've come to realize that it's not going to fall out of the sky and land in my lap because I've been through a lot in life. I have to bust my butt and tap in. If I'm willing to do that and put it all on the line and make sacrifices, I can have anything I put my mind to. Wholeheartedly, I believe that God wants the best for me but I feel he's not going to just sit back and say "you know what, Micah's had a tough one. Let me throw him a few blessings... You really have to be careful when talking to people who live their lives defeated. They haven't learned to see past life's pain, or as my grandmother used to say, "They Haven't learned How To Dance In The Rain". They do see what could be, they're just stuck where they are. You can't control someone's lack of belief. It's wise not to waste time explaining the "Possibilities". Whoever wants to understand how to elevate, trust me, they'll either figure it out or begin to ask questions. Believe it or not, successful people are motivated by other successful people. It's unsuccessful that seem to be intimidated. It's very rare that you'll be criticized by someone doing more than you've done. Don't ever forget that!

Throughout life, seasons fade and it's up to us to know when time is up. For example, if you stay too long in a relationship that is turning toxic, the harder it will be for you to cut it off. If you are overextending to bring consistent comfort to an individual who needs to be blended out of your life, at the discomfort of your own purpose you're cheating yourself. Knowing when to leave is just as important as knowing to stay or engage in a relationship of any kind.

Taking time away is a good way to gain a clearer perspective and fade away unhealthy attachments. For me, a good 45 minute commute to work with the windows down and some good music playing while focusing on my breathing is how I digress. It's definitely good for your mental health. Getting away from the hustle and bustle of life's grind and just changing scenery a little bit, changing the pace of your day. Escaping the chaos for just a bit. Focusing on life's blessings and gaining gratitude for those blessings.

It's not good to see the same corners, stoplights, people, and buildings at all times. Just getting out of your comfort zone and adjusting the scenery a little bit, makes a world of a difference. Doing something new takes willingness along with flexibility. Anyone who isn't willing to get out of their own comfort zone eventually limits how far they can go in any situation. It's not hard to limit your thinking. If you're not careful, you can become a limited liability. Perhaps along my journey, I've allowed too many folks to just sit in the boat and not paddle. Are you carrying some dead weight while attempting to pursue your goals? Are people in your sphere of influence just along for the ride? Have you accepted their complacency while unconsciously stagnating your own journey?

To be blunt, I have been guilty of all of the above at some point in my life. Possibly, it held me back. Being around people with a lack of vision, stunted my vision. I stayed at my first shop for seven years. I did that because I made that shop part of my plan. Never forming a plan of my own until later. It's very possible that I may have not even seen the possibilities fading of what could be because of familiarity.

Even here, recently I visited a property, two stories about 4,000 square feet, the gentleman wanted to sell or lease. I'm talking it over with my pops, and I was like the cost of the property is $500,000 dollars. He says, "Son, that's half a million dollars." I reply, "Yeah, it is." He looks at me and says, "Do you have it?" Without hesitation, I say, "No I don't." Taking caution he says, "I don't know if I'd do that son, that's a lot of money." I respect my dad's opinion, but immediately, my mind went to, what it is going to take to get it! Let's pray about it. If it's God's will, he'll provide a way. The immediate reaction was that's half a million dollars. Don't get me wrong, I understood where my pops were coming from, especially based on where I came from. Nobody in our family has ever had that kind of money because that's our story. That's what we're going to stick to. I don't know about you but I refuse to just succumb to what was. The old me is fading and a new me who wants to live life unrestricted has emerged. My prayer for you reading now is that you move beyond what you used to be able to do or what it looked like before you started reading this book. Let's really dig deep and see what's out there. Best believe there is an entirely new world you and I haven't even tapped into or scratched the surface of. Permit yourself to change the dynamic of your family.

Please take a minute to vision cast and dream with me. I'm thinking beyond the barbershop like if we close the shop, let's open a male tailoring suit shop and still call it TaylorMade. We'll suit you from bow ties to necktie, shirts, cufflinks, jackets, pants, belts, shoes, wingtips, wide toes, whatever you want. We'll even sell you some cologne on the way out the door. We're going to really tailor you up. Just imagine your dreams becoming reality. Don't rush, take a few moments to simply picture it in your mind. If you can think of it, you can become or have it. My friend, we don't really have that option if we're not putting ourselves in a position to win.

There is more to my vision than just cutting hair. I've had to learn the hard way that I can't open up my vision to just anybody Even my closest family because not everybody is going to get it and not everyone is going to support it or understand it. With that being said, I just learned to fade out and tuck it tight and give it to God, letting him take the lead. Truth be told, some people will only believe in your vision after it's complete and you'll just have to invite the naysayers to the ribbon-cutting ceremony. Perhaps they'll believe in the power of dreaming someday, but until then you got to keep pushing with your head down and your focus sharp. In the lyrics of Caron Wheeler and Soul II Soul "Keep on moving, don't stop, like Click -Clock, find your own way to stay the time will come one day…"

New Barbers

One of the fundamental things I had to learn from fading from the old and blending into the new was in order to build I couldn't do it alone. With that said, my ultimate desire is to build a culture and I set out to do just that. In the process, I ask the barbers I'm interviewing to bring at least a portfolio or some social media pics of their past cuts. Even before they're allowed on the floor of the shop, we do at least a week, potentially two weeks of shadowing and training. The idea or purpose of observing is not to micromanage or that I doubt the skill of the individual it is to assure the barber fits or blends in with the culture we are creating. Before you can get in the rotation of being one of the barbers, I give you a few cuts, let you go at it, and I come back and look it over and critique it. If I like your quality we keep going, I don't just bring you in because you're a barber and you have a license or you're able to pay me booth rent. Truthfully, if I take your booth rent money, there's a lot that comes along with that. There's a responsibility that comes along with that exchange. Money has a person's energy attached to it. If your energy isn't right, now that energy's in my wallet, now I'm carrying that around wherever I go, good, bad or ugly, it might just completely derail my plan. I'm sure you heard the quote "All money isn't good money".

Being intentional about seeing who's coming in and what their plans are is a must in successfully running a business. For instance, I just hired a guy fresh out of school. His dad wanted to put together his own shop; which I thought was pretty dope. Instead of taking his dad up on the offer, he decides to initially work for me and spend more time perfecting his craft. I was honored that wanted to get equipped from me before he just jumped out there and took a chance which may or may not worked. He's humble enough to realize that he needed training, to me, that's a major plus because it shows humility and a lack of pride. I hired him because I admire those characteristics. That to me was a green light that I can work with this dude because he's coachable. Having the ability to be coached is a way to secure longevity in any field and barbering is not exempt.

Now I can walk him through the process and if and when I have to call him out a little bit, he's not going to be offended. He's going to be open to constructive criticism. I love being hands-on with the hiring process and holding barber's hands for the first few weeks and walking them through the expectations of TaylorMade. It's not just about them getting clients or barbers making money. It is about them making clients happy and retaining clients and keeping the standard of the shop held high. Ultimately, it is up to me to fade the lines or barriers assuring everything is blended in the business when the shop lights are on and off at TaylorMade. I'll fade away or blend out any potential threat to my dream. My dream is worth protecting.

CHAPTER FIVE:
THE LINEUP

What I've learned about the lineup is that you can have a crisp edge up and it'll make a bad haircut look good. On the other hand, if you have a barber who cuts too far into a customer's hairline, it can make that good fade I mentioned in the previous chapter look horrible. Many barbers miss the key point of the shape-up. The finishing touches add to the overall experience of the haircut. Taking time to polish your work, while helping your client feel proud about their purchase. Having a sense of pride in being a craftsman, loving each step of the process.

Although this may or may not be the last step for a barber during the haircutting process, it is the most vital. Try thinking of this in a different light, if you hire someone for landscaping and they leave the edges untrimmed and misaligned. Wouldn't an unhedged lawn that is freshly cut stick out like a sore thumb? Let's just say you hired a painter, who paints your house well but does a patchy job with the borders. How would you think the house would look in the end? The frightening thing is that many clients leave their perspective barbershops with haircuts misaligned or after their money has been collected.

This bears repeating; not that we're trying to cheat the process, but a strong line saves a bad haircut. If the cut's good, but the line is bad, the whole thing is just sloppy. Certain things that are more commonly used weren't as common when I first got started cutting, such as enhancements. Barbers in the industry now, regularly use dyes or color enhancers, fibers, and even hair units. I have learned the correct way to apply them, simply because some of my clients not only prefer the look, but they are also willing to pay extra for that additional service. It's important to be a barber that's versatile. Being able to provide a wide arrange of services upon request. Everybody wants that fresh off the movie scene look, and I get that, I get it with no judgment. I'm a barber that isn't the greatest by any means, but I've learned to master my craft. I say this having had years of observation and seeing haircutting from so many different perspectives. To a degree, a lot of the younger stylists that are coming out of barber school today are hiding their true potential behind these enhancements. As a young barber myself, we didn't have access to modern-day technology. Not only did I not have a cell phone, there were no computers with internet access in my home. Having a powerful tool such as YouTube at a young age would've been the ultimate advantage. Something that I could've studied for free, at my own convenience. I've met barbers that have never spent a day in a Barber Academy but instead, learned their trade by watching tutorials online. Right, Wrong or Indifferent; the information is out there for anyone willing to learn literally anything. Not just barbering, you can learn how to change an entire Transmission in your car, watching enough internet content.

In the early 90s, if you couldn't cut, you just couldn't cut and if you misaligned the edge up, there was no camouflaging it. Some folks reading this book know exactly what I mean and may have had to wear a few hats until their hairline grew back. The only way to adjust mistakes back then, where to wait for your hairline to grow completely back in. Nowadays, you can spray and hide your imperfections. In those days, a lineup exposed your skillset. If you couldn't cut, the evidence would show in your lineup, literally.

Now, let's apply this same line up principle to life in general. Outside of the physical lineup, the mindset or shape up of the people around you in your circle is extremely important. Someone stated, "If you show me who you hang around I can predict your future". The way I see it, the people you surround yourself with have the potential of having a huge impact on your personal energy and outlook on life. People either fuel you, drain you or sustain you. Depending on your current level of comfort, it's very rare that you'll experience a grey area. People shouldn't fall in your circle, they should be there for a purpose. That purpose should never be to just take up space. I'll take it a step further; individuals will help elevate you in life if they are meant to be in your inner circle. Take a deep breath and think for a minute who you have in your line up, in your core group. Does your inner circle fall in line with your purpose or destiny? Trust me, I'm not just putting you on the spot when I ask this question because I've had to do my own self-inventory and overall evaluation of the people consuming my time on more than one occasion. Do this unapologetically, your greater future self depends on it. Nobody is responsible for your personal growth but you. You need people who will water your seed, not set fire to it. It's very important that the people around you are goal-oriented and have similar interests in what you want out of life. The Good Book says that iron sharpens iron. That couldn't be any further from the truth.

Considering I'm a sole proprietor now, being able to control who I work around at the shop is a complete game changer. In the past, I had to succumb to a lot of unnecessary tension and a lack of teamwork. Obviously, I didn't want to deal with this but had to simply because I rented the booth and had no control over what type of energy I worked around. My friends, in my earlier days, I couldn't control the lineup of the individuals that I shared space with at work. During that time, I just had to learn to tune out certain things just to get through my day.

Eventually, I found myself going to work and just reading in between haircuts. I've always enjoyed conversations with my customers but after a while, it began to feel like I didn't share the same interest in barbering as my coworkers. Not that my way is "the way', I was just 20yrs younger than both of them and very much interested in expanding the business whereas they were more interested in maintaining what we had. Which wasn't necessarily a bad concept because we had built a great business. However, in life, Change is Inevitable but growth is Optional. Nothing in life stays the same, you either grow through the times or simply go through them. During that period, I felt like I had reached a pivotal point in my career. I felt as if I was just going to work simply to provide for my family, instead of seeing what my license had to offer me. There are so many different levels of barbering, and I had only seen one. My inner entrepreneur kept pulling on my heart strings making it hard to be ok with good. It was almost like the hair enhancements that I spoke about earlier, simply hiding what really existed. I became completely out of tune with the shop at that point. Literally, I was just blocking everyone out because we were not on the same page. At that time, it felt as if I was being ridiculed for digging deep and trying to be as successful as possible. Without a doubt, I know you can identify with me if you've ever made your mind up to chase your dreams. If you are locked into your goals but shallow people are attacking you for wanting to go deeper in life, it's in your best interest to change scenery. By doing so I'm not promising you that you won't face opposition, however, until you do so, you'll never know what could be.

To avoid negative thinking, I lined up with different books and tried to educate myself throughout my workday on things I need to work on. Choosing to align with things that were going to make me a better barber, a greater husband, a better father, and a greater person. Discovering one of the greatest gems I could ever give myself was self-alignment. There are times when you are between appointments, and you glance in the mirror at yourself and come to realize you need a shape up yourself, but all the stylist in the shop are occupied. The skillset is second nature, so you remember you have the capacity to do for yourself as you do for others. Without pause, you grab your trimmers, look into the mirror at the right angles and line yourself up. The barbers reading this book at this moment will find value in this line above and totally get my drift. Those brief moments of self-care are priceless. There's something special about a fresh cut.

Aligning myself bettered my faith and gave all of my problems to God. Not trying to hash things out and fix things myself, whether I'm the booth renter or the shop owner I give God all my cares and that's the bottom line. Even now as the sole proprietor of my own business, there is a line I can cross and things that I can't control, but God can. Once you turn things over to him, you have to trust that everything will work out according to his will for your life.

Note, I can set the business up and uphold the standards, but there's a lot of spiritual warfare out here and things that come your way that you can't even see. Problems at times are just like oxygen, we can't see it with our natural eyes but that doesn't delete the reality that it's all around us. The great thing is that we're fighting a fixed fight and God has never lost a battle, pound for pound undefeated champion of the Universe. Daily, I book my appointment with God and He gives me a fresh cut and a flawless shape up. Spending time with him helps create the tone for my day.

You've got to choose to line up with God and His plan for your life. If not, you're subjecting yourself to all kinds of attacks from the enemy. Wars are won with armies, and you need the army of God as well as the armor of God on you. Life is a battlefield. Remember, being lined up correctly is the difference between an epic victory and a destructive failure. If your team is not right, if your head space is not correct, if your faith is not right, you're not lined up. You're not in a position to get a 100% of what could be if you are halfway lined up. There is no such thing as a halfway shape up, it's either all or nothing. Take a chance on God's plan for your life, and realize that He's already taken a chance on you. Line everything up precisely, and the finished product will literally blow your mind. In the shop, we use the term "Crispy".

Adjusting Hairlines

As a barber, I serve customers with receding hairlines. From having dealt with hair lost from a first-hand perspective, I keep it real with them. Simply, I tell them man that's halfway to the back, this might be time to let it all go. Explaining to them that hair loss isn't the end all. This is what I tell them to let me turn you on toward a hot towel shave, pore cleansing/ hot towel treatment, with the lemon grass, and give yourself some time to breathe in clean relaxing air. Let me turn you into a different dynamic of the service you've never experienced because you never shaved your head or your face. Now we're going into this new phase of your style. I'm going to show you a different level of self-care. Another option is the Man Unit, which is a real hot right in the industry right now and also known as a better version of the toupee. Depending on the style and application, it last four to five months if done right. There are other alternatives but the greatest thing I can ever encourage someone to do is to adjust and find themselves within themselves.

Somebody that might not want to shave their hair off completely can literally transform their entire image, using hair units, I can take a client with a bald head and give him waves, and have him feeling like he's 25 again. I've cut hair for a really long time and what I've learned most is that a minor adjustment or enhancement gives the client a different level of confidence and optimism. It's amazing that a mere haircut can do wonders for a person's self-esteem. Seeing them walk out the door with their head high, shoulders back, chest out, ready to take on life man. The process is not to be taken lightly, there's power in a cut. The power of that adjustment, that tweak totally shifts confidence. Most likely, an individual feels less confident if there not on their A game, especially if the haircut isn't tailored to fit them.

When you're not being yourself in life, you are imitating the best version of someone else. It is impossible to truly be someone else no matter how hard you try. The best impression of someone outside of being yourself is still second best and remains an impersonation. Be you and you'll win every time. There's true power in the essence of originality. You were born an original, it's important that you don't die a copy. Find your standard and maintain that standard. Tailor and Custom fit your character, let it be the signature between every transaction for the rest of your life. Leave a lasting impression of your true self, not a carbon copy.

Enhancements and other additives create a level of luxury service. It's key to remember that enhancements are merely meant to supplement the service. I can only enhance what's already there and it's up to the client to see their true value before and after the haircut. Although a nice crisp haircut adds a certain value to anyone's day, it's true that the Man makes the haircut; the haircut doesn't make the man. Say this with me KEEP YOUR HEAD ON STRAIGHT.

In some cases, you don't feel like you're the best version of yourself when your hair is in question. It is one of my jobs to make the client feel comfortable in their own skin. Being a barber is similar to being a coach. My intent while a customer is in my chair is to help them look in the mirror and see a portrait of their best self. Going through the service, I ask a series of questions. What we're doing with your hair today? Is there a certain style that you're looking for or do you trust my creativity? By chance, have you considered doing a man unit? I still have to converse with the client and encourage them while I'm servicing and building them up. As their barber/counselor, my words have life, and I want to do more than just book your next service so that you come back and get adjusted. My goal is to make sure that you take something from the experience that goes far deeper than the haircut itself. The ultimate desire is that when they get up from my chair and leave my shop, they won't feel comfortable just sitting in another random barber's seat or going to a random shop for convenience's sake. Providing an ongoing experience is truly what I aim for in serving my clients.

Well after the haircut, I envision clients saying "I got to see my dude Micah man. He gives me life when I get a cut. The haircuts are clean, the cuts are consistent". The conversation is the most valuable part of the exchange. Creating a memory that lingers with the customer is the next level. Giving them a sense of motivation and support is superior service. Fresh Wind, as I like to call it. To anyone inspired to be in business and taking the time to read this book, here is some food for thought. If you book appointments only, you can make money but if you build relationships, you'll have lifelong customers with built-in relationships. Relationships can potentially take you to an entirely different dimension in life.

A barber can be booked and busy but fails to forge true relationships and direct lines to their clients. Clients that sit in my chair are going to walk away with more than a line up. I'm giving these customers a chance to see what could be. While cutting hair, I'm digging into their soul and exposing their potential, and encouraging them on a level that they've never gotten in their entire life. Again, not because I'm so special or great is because I want to be a line up and down line. My philosophy is even if the cut is better elsewhere, your conversation can't hold a candle to what we're building on over here. Cut and conversations are all encompassing. It's a package deal. The fact of the matter is I serve my customers. I don't want to cut just random people. Not that I have a problem servicing whoever comes through my door, I just prefer to build with people who want to grow.

In the words of the great philosopher Nas, "Death To The Pessimistic Mind State, lack of hope, low spirited & low self-esteemed individuals." Abundant living should be the mission.

I'll do walk-ins. I'll do what it takes to keep my business flowing but I don't want you in my chair just because you've heard I do a good haircut. When I'm booked up, you're going to jump in the next barber's chair. I want to cut folk that appreciates my style of service. Not just me personally but the barbers that I work with as well, the entire establishment. Once you fall in love with the ambiance of being TaylorMade, then I know you're here for the long haul. You're not just here for convenience's sake, and you won't ever have an issue with promoting the brand because you've become a lifelong client. In turn, you're compelled to refer people who appreciate the same type of customer survive as you do. Now we have a community of people on the same line of the page. Then we're all lined up.

Testimonials

I know someone who has been talking about writing a book, his name is Cameron Crawford. He's a cancer survivor and before he even got a chance to tell me his full story, I saw the best in him. I said dude, your story is incredible. Mr. Crawford, I said you've inspired me as a barber, as well as a friend, and somebody can literally get something valuable from your story. You need to put it on paper. He says, "I've thought about it, but I don't think I should. What if nobody reads it?" No, I'm not going to let you do that man. Since you're in my chair right now, I'm going to hold you to that standard. Don't look at it like if I write it nobody will read it, your life is a story of God's love, and literally what he can do through any kind of circumstance.

When people hear the term cancer, they think death sentence, and you beat cancer brother. You're a survivor. Mr. Crawford, other people battling cancer could read your book and just get a second wind, a fresh start. By the time I was done, Mr. Crawford jumped out of the chair and stood to his feet, and said, "You know what? I'm writing a book." Since then, he's sent me four texts over two days like, "Man, point me in the right direction. How do I get started? What is it going to take? What do I need to do?" It's important to make proper use of your words and know just how powerful words are. That's just one small example, a testimony of a situation in the barber chair, but I've had two customers in the past month who are signing up for barber school. Barbers are more than just service providers, we are influencers.

Two of my customers never ever considered barbering, let alone going to school for it. They were just working dead-end jobs and not feeling fulfilled. Not even feeling confident in the ability to cut hair, but me just saying, "You know what dude? Read this. If you can watch testimonials on YouTube, you can learn the craft of barbering." Then seeing that light bulb goes off in their head, that aha moment, then taking that chance or leap of faith. The two customers ended up graduating from barber school just to see if they have what it takes to be a barber.

Anyone Can Cut Hair

Anybody can do anything if they're dedicated. Firmly believe that dedication is the fundamental to learning anything. Most people are not lined up with the right people and are not fed the things that ignite them to move toward their dreams and aspirations. They're not fed what could be they are starved by hearing what they cannot achieve. The masses are fed doubt about their potential to do something great. Outside of people, if you turn on enough TV or listen to segments of the news, or especially scroll through social media, you'll be defeated without even knowing you're defeated. Societal norms and stigmas blind us from staying in the lines of our greatness and position us to look out at what everyone else is doing around us. Media stuff often times weakens the spirit and kills their potential and dreams.

Believe me when I say lining up truly happens when one comes to grips with the fact that we have been unaligned. It is impossible to fix something in your life that you can't see or discern that something is broken. Check to see what lines up in your life. Anything that is out of place or misaligned in your life can be adjusted. Before you can truly serve in business, you must connect the dots to your own life. Don't forget to run a gut check on yourself and focus on self -service. The best business advantage is customer service.

CHAPTER SIX:
CUSTOMER SERVICE

Customer service can be a make or break in business. Let's examine this scenario. If I'm a waiter or a waitress and I'm working in a restaurant, if the food is subpar or not up to standard but I can give you excellent customer service, more than likely, you'll forget about how bad your food tasted and give us another chance. If the steak was not cooked the way you wanted it to be, and I have it remade for you and bring it right back but it's still tough; I have to exhaust ever option possible to ensure that your experience meets your expectation. I have to put myself aside. Whatever I may be going through has to take a back seat and I dive head first into what your needs are as a customer. You came here to be served. You came here because you didn't feel like cooking at home with a pile of dishes waiting for you after dinner. Although you came to eat, the ambiance and environment are just as important to why you came out in the first place. Customers want to feel not only important but valued as well.

In a relation to barbering, you came here because you can't cut your hair. Well, if you are able to cut your own hair, you don't feel like cutting it today. So, you came here for me to do it. You came here to be pampered a little bit. So as your barber, I have to be mindful of that. The one thing that I constantly reiterate to my barbers is the importance of punctuality. If you're going to set appointments, be sure you can cut the cut in a minimum 30 minute gap. Be sure that you're on time in between those time slots. Make sure you're not just rushing through the service. Again, you have to have time to break your tools down and properly sanitize everything. So be sure to allow time in your schedule and in between your appointments to do that. It's vital to the overall health of the public that you do this regularly. Make it a part of your routine until it becomes second nature. Something that you no longer have to put any thought into.

You've got to have balance. You have to be able to know that you can make the schedule or better yet the customer's time, the main focus. It's important to make sure the environment has a vibe. For instance, I'm a lover of music, I absolutely love music. I love all genres of music, literally. Not everyone has to be a lover of music but if you notice almost every business uses some sort of background music to add to the overall ambiance they're trying to create. If I'm the customer and I walk into an establishment and hear this awkward dead silence, no clippers humming, no television noise or talking, I personally feel like it takes away from the overall experience. Even when companies advertise commercials on television, they use music to make their product stick in your head a little better. For example, McDonalds uses a certain melody in their adds when they say, "Ba da, bah bah Bah....I'm lovin it!" I'm almost certain that you heard that specific melody in your head as you read, "Ba da. Bah bah Bah" They even have a term for this music usage, they're called jingles. For whatever reason, music adds value to the whole experience. Jingles are used in just about every commercial on television and radio add.

A good vibe feels something like, Family Feud playing in the background or Maxwell singing a dope melody. It needs to be a comfortable, relaxing environment where if the customer does have a wait time, it doesn't seem exhausting. I'm enjoying the good vibe. I'm enjoying the conversations that I'm hearing. I'm enjoying the potential education that I'm getting. I've overheard young cats getting schooled by older cats in my lobby on numerous occasions, and getting the opportunity to witness a young man sitting there soaking up knowledge from a senior citizen is a powerful thing. That's rare, especially considering nowadays it's not as common to see knowledge passed from generation to generation specifically in urban communities. I recently had to chew out a few of my barbers over the usage of profanity. In order to help drive my point home I've created a cuss cup. Now they have to pay for unprofessionalism. Mainly because it's my namesake that's taking a hit. If I'm getting off work and receiving messages from customers that didn't even sit in my chair, complaining about another barber's inappropriate language in front of their child; the overall customer service is horrible. Specifically, I'm paying for another barber's carelessness.

The haircut could be great, but the usage of poor language and vulgarity hurts the overall moral of the shop. That's completely inconsiderate of the client and their time in your chair but specifically in my barbershop. It's ok to talk openly with a customer. If you grew up around them that's one thing but in a shop setting, you never know who could be walking through that door. You have no idea who's in the building or who they are connected to. Clients can easily add to your books with referrals or take away from them with complaints. You could be cutting the president of the university across the street. Or even the owner of a multi-million dollar corporation. We recently had the regional vice president of Subway in town checking on a location across the street. While in town, he paid us a visit and got a quick clean up. Considering Subway is one of our corporate partners for our annual Back to School Bash, he fed the whole shop and brought us all free subs, chips, cookies, and drinks. "Hey guys, I just want to thank you for what you do in the local community. Thank you for choosing us as a partner." Let's say for instance that he comes in to feed the crew and overhears cussing and vulgar language with every breath of the barber's conversation. It would immediately make him think twice about associating his brand with such unprofessionalism. Especially considering their brand is worldwide.

Mr. Peter Toomey will sit in the first available seat when he comes in, so my new barbers have no idea of our partnership. He doesn't come in announcing titles, he simply comes back with a truck load of free food for my crew with a huge smile. A gesture that will always be appreciated. Whenever a client leaves their chair, I remind them that they may be cutting Executives of major corporations. On any given work day, as a barber, you can literally meet somebody who can completely expand your network and change the direction of your career.

I recently met with the director who oversees a local boy's home. I think up to about 50 boys within their program conveniently they needed a barber. So now we've got a contract to go cut their hair. Well, if my customer service is not up to par and my communication is not A1, that potential contract could be in jeopardy. I don't even fit the criteria of being a potential candidate. If I'm talking about how Young Jeezy beat Gucci Mane in their most recent rap battle, I'm immediately disqualifying myself from a different level of clientele. You've got to know when it's appropriate and when it's not, feel the vibe and let them talk. You listen and respond according to how the conversation goes.

So I think customer service is right up there with the lineup. Earlier on, I mentioned that a good lineup could save a bad haircut. Good customer service can save a bad haircut as well. If the service is good, they'll come back and give you a second chance in a lot of cases. But if the cut is bad and the service is bad, there's a good chance that you're done and that's not just in barbering. That holds true in a lot of fields. Customer service has to be made a priority when dealing with the public.

Clientele

I've cut a few movie stars, a few professional athletes, a TV personality, local politicians, as well as the president of a neighboring major university. Those experiences have been cool, but I get more out of cutting the common man, the 9:00 to 5:00 man. The man going through an uphill battle. I get more of a charge when cutting them and hearing their story because their story in a lot of cases is my story. I can relate to them the most. I can't really relate to people who have it all because in my opinion success is a journey, it's not a destination. That's why we have to cherish the time we've been given. One of my favorite clients to date recently passed away, Mr. AJ Johnson.

He played Ezell in the movie Friday, produced by; Ice Cube. Great energy and an even better personality. I've had the privilege of cutting some of the guys off of the TV show Wild "N" Out, that's cool to put on a resume, but the young man who plays fourth-grade football, who's considered a barber, I'm his biggest fan. I'm moved by him the most. Like, "I want his autograph." That's what does it for me man, are people who have similar stories and similar starting points and want the same things out of life, so to speak. Not to say that I don't relate to the high profiled clients, because most of them have some pretty intense journeys themselves. It's just that the drive and optimism of a young dreamer encourage me and give me hope for a better future.

If Taylor Made were a vehicle, it would be a Cadillac

I'm biased, I'm a lover of the pristine design and comfort of a Cadillac. Car manufacturers never say, "it drives like a Porsche". Instead, we've all heard high end vehicles be compared to the drive of a Cadillac. It's almost as if Cadillac is the standard, although Cadillac is not a Mercedes. Mercedes in the luxury line is up there. Audi is up there. Lexus is up there, but they'll say, "Man, this Lexus drives like a Cadillac." The way it rides is unlike any other automobile on the road. Your commute is so much smoother and enjoyable. No one likes a bumpy ride.

When you're sitting in a Lac, it's different. Your transition from point A to point B is more like floating than driving. The ride. It's the ride. You feel like you're in luxury. When you hit a bump, you float through the bump man. You don't boom, bang, boom. You don't rumble through the bumps in the road, you're going to flow with them all. I say Cadillac because to me, it's a bit personal. Not only have I owned a few in my lifetime, but ironically, I owned my favorite make and model while enrolled in barber school. I went to take my barber's exam in a 1991 Pearl White Cadillac Deville with a burgundy interior.

I rode for about six hours to Richmond Virginia, and that was one of the most liberating road trips of my life. I turned on Frankie Beverly/Maze, Sam Cooke, Bobby Womack, Marvin Gaye, Rufus, The O'Jays, The Whispers and I put the car in cruise control. I set it to 65, although the speed limit is 70 all the way up interstate I-81N. I did this to ensure that anybody in a hurry would zip on by me because I was intentionally taking in the entire journey. I stayed in the right-hand lane the whole way. And brother, I just drifted all the way up the coast. I took my time and wasn't worried about anything. Nothing in this world. I kept going over the steps to my practical exam in my head. I was in my Lac and in my zone on my way to complete the certification for my Master Barber License. I literally floated all the way from Greeneville TN to Richmond VA. I arrived at the Hotel where the test would take place the night before, just to ensure no issues the day of. I got a good nine hours of sleep and ate a continental breakfast downstairs. It was an amazing feeling to be completely prepared instead of nervous and not ready.

We didn't get confirmation rather we passed or failed but I just knew I had, I felt it in my heart simply because I poured every ounce of effort and energy into that one moment in time. Although the look I got from my prompters said otherwise. Their body language and evil stares made it look as if I had failed. Matter of fact, I remember the guy beside me warning me that he had taken the practical exam five times. He said, "Man you were sweating so hard that some of the perspiration got on your stuff, they'll fail you for that. Trust me I know" I just looked at him and smiled, I wasn't hearing what he was saying though. I knew I had passed, I felt it internally. In fact, once I packed up my belongings, I drove straight to the beach, man. I got in my Cadillac and I just kept driving in the opposite direction of home. Once I got to the coast, I got out of my car and I walked on that sand, and just stood there. I felt the wind blowing with the smell of salt water all around me, and I listened to the wave's crash. That was one of the best trips of my life man. I don't recall every feeling more accomplished in my entire life. Working a graveyard shift while enrolled in the barber academy, the journey was intense, to say the least.

When I rode back, I wasn't perturbed that it was a seven and a half hour trip. I just, again, enjoyed the fact that I accomplished something that potentially could change my life. I had worked and waited my entire life to find a purpose and profession that I not only enjoyed but could be proud of. I blocked out all the what if's and waited patiently for my score to be mailed. Once I got that letter in the mail and saw that I had scored a 97, I cried. I still to this day haven't met any barber to score that high on the last part of the examination. Not to say that it's never been done, I've just not personally met anyone.

As I mentioned before, I drove up the night before. All of my tests weren't until 10 o'clock that morning. I got to my hotel at seven o'clock the night before. I got nine hours of sleep. I got to the testing site an hour and a half before the time for it to start. So, there are no flat tires or no potential headache, migraine, absolutely nothing can stop this mission. I was in that Lac, we floated up to Virginia and floated back to Tennessee. That ride was a complete vibe within itself. I've done everything in my power since that day to capture that vibe and make it my own. The TaylorMade Vibe is a place of peace and comfort. So, I would definitely say Taylor Made is a Cadillac. You're sitting on leather, on your way to a premium level of grooming. The perfect destination.

Personal Experience With Customer Service

In my personal experience with customer service, what works and what doesn't work is just more or less attention to detail. In the shop that I worked in before I opened my own shop, the barbers kind of did their own thing as far as their hours. If they set appointments, they had it to where the customers kind of bent to their schedules instead of the other way around. One thing I learned just as a young barber in that shop was seeing how they managed their schedules and handled their clientele. I had the distinct privilege of hearing all their clients' backlash, complaints, and everything that wasn't right about the full service. Things they would rarely say to their barber, but considering I was usually the first one to open up shop, I heard all the jawing and nagging. The cut might've been fire, but it took too long to get in the chair.

That's setting a bad tone for not only that specific customer but the shop as a whole. That customer can go to the public and spread the bad word about the business and lack of customer service. Customers don't care about your personal needs or what you have going on throughout the day. They come for service and often times to vent to their barber. So just piggybacking off of those experiences and in comparison to my own business, I've let barbers go for bad customer service. It's hard to build business credibility but way too easy to kill it. One specific gentleman I hired from Miami, Florida, was literally one of the best barbers I've ever seen in my life. Crazy talent. Crazy, crazy talent. Could fade, could dread, could braid. I mean, could color, could highlight, could texturize. Anything hair specific, he could not only do it, but he mastered it. But because he was so good, he let his skillset rob him of quality customer service.

I kind of overextended our relationship a little bit because of his amazing skillset. Silly me, I allowed him seven no calls no shows. I soon learned that by accepting this gentleman for his talent and giving him a pass, I'm literally taking my brand and flushing it down the toilet. A quality cutter and craftsman should also exhibit good customer service, especially a veteran barber. One thing I've never been a fan of is dealing with the attitude of another barbers client. As a customer, you don't even sit in my chair but now I'm the complaint department. The streets are talking and they're saying Taylormade doesn't really care about keeping up with appointments. So I've had to make to pretty hard decisions in order to protect the overall integrity of the brand I've built. Again, someone who initially added a lot of spunk and a lot of precision to the team. I mean, brought in a fair amount of clientele without knowing a soul. Moving hear from another state and building a network quickly. When I say we were jumping not only eight hours a day, 10 hours a day and constant flow of traffic.

My journey has taught me that skilled barbers can bring in a lot of people, but skilled barbers with bad habits can run off a lot of people in the same regard. Don't give people permission to ruin what you've built with sweat equity. I'll try to do my best when I set an appointment to be at least ready and prepared 15, no less than 10 minutes prior to the scheduled time. So if you book for 9:00, I'm ready to rock at 8:50. But in the same regard, if a customer is a no-call no-show or continuously shows up late, I've refused services in the past because there has to be some kind of a balance between the customer and the barber. Time is valuable. If you're my next appointment and you're running late, you're backing me up the rest of the day for all the rest of my other appointments. If they're early or on time, it's not fair to them that I'm running behind because of your tardiness.

So I've also incorporated a no-call, no-show fee. You have to pay a percentage, so you are kind of more mindful of not being late. Also encouraging the barbers as well, if we're late we have to dock something off the haircut. You can't just say, "My bad." We've got to give them the same respect with their time. We can't just charge them for being late, if we're late we have to abide by the same rule. Just learning what works and what doesn't. In regards to customer service, I've learned that a bad haircutter who is polished with phenomenal customer service can not only make it in this industry but can grow tremendously. I've hired here recently in the past year, a lot of students who are fresh out of school. These individuals have not only excelled, but they also handle constructive criticism extremely well. Not to say that a veteran barber can't work, but my experiences in the past came with a lot of ego and drama that I don't really have patience for...

My message to the younger barbers is "the quality of the cut comes in time". If you can master customer service along the way while you're getting polished, you'll be just fine. If you go into it head first, just focusing on making sure your haircuts are clean but you don't even communicate to them, you're missing the big picture. Or if you do talk to them but you're short with them because you have something going on with your family or the kids are tripping, now you bringing that attitude into the workplace with you. Now, they're feeling the tension and the energy, that all goes in the same bubble with customer service. Your customer doesn't want to hear about your problems. The customer sits in the chair to tell the barber his or her problems.

I was learning how to separate personal life, professional life, good days, bad days, what have you. I think that this is a nucleus for what good customer service is supposed to look like. Making the customer the main priority, giving them your undivided attention while being punctual as well as professional. And with those qualities, I've seen it work time and time again. Even with my current crew being fresh out of school, not polished but definitely have all the tangible skills of excellent customer service. Without question, they have a high ceiling in this industry. Good energy is a key ingredient to a well-balanced barbershop. Working with fellow barbers who share the same sentiments for the craft. This produces not only a positive working environment, but it also provides a healthy space for the community as a whole to grow and evolve.

There's a method to barbering, especially for those fresh out of school. Whenever your chair is empty, smile and greet every client in the building. Eventually, if for no other reason than convenience, those very clients will patronize your chair. The same people that may have overlooked you or simply preferred another barber's style, will be in your chair. Being approachable versus sitting around with a mean mug on your face. If I'm the customer and you as the barber don't look the slightest bit interested in cutting my hair, I wouldn't want you to cut my hair. I tell my barbers all the time, customers can feel the energy you produce, make it good energy. So just seeing them getting those things adhering to my advice and taking head while growing and learning, it really is refreshing. So I know for a fact that customer service is right up there next to that sharp line on a crisp haircut. The quality of the cut is equally important but you really can't have one without the other. It's a package deal.

Customer service is prioritizing your time and your attention in a way that it benefits the customer. Focusing on them first and you second. Making sure their needs are met while making sure that you're intentional about making them your main priority. Attention to not only the detail of the haircut but the detail of the conversation as well. Be present during the service, don't rob the client of a potential experience of a lifetime. Make a first-time customer choose you to be their personal barber and book with you weekly or even bi-weekly. Building with the community and connecting with various walks of life while exchanging energy through a grooming session, that's the true essence of Barbering at its finest.

I know how to respond to you and reason with you. I can't go at you raw and rash. I can't go at you hostile. Boss or no boss, you don't have authority over people. Business or no business, you have to learn to deal with people respectfully, even if they don't deal with you respectfully, you've got to learn to give them that initial respect first. You are only responsible for your own actions and character. Set the tone when dealing with the public. Be the thermostat, or they'll make you a fluctuating thermometer. Stay in a positive mental space and disregard any potential negative energy from people. Every day is a new adventure, and sometimes, life will throw a few curveballs at you simply because people can be unpredictable at times. Never let unpredictable times determine your level of accomplishment. Life is ten percent, what happens to you while the ninety percent is what you do about it!

Satisfied Clients

I can tell if a customer is satisfied. They not only come back on a weekly basis, but they tell people, they bring people, they promote me on their social media outlets and they advertise for me. Those acts of kindness save me hundreds, maybe even thousands of dollars that would be used for advertisements. For instance, I rented a billboard recently which cost me 750 for one month. That's a lot of money to spend considering most folk in traffic usually look at their phones more than the road, signs, or billboards. So I'm paying almost $800 for something that may or may not be beneficial. Versus a satisfied customer, from what I've learned in business is the best form of advertisement. It's easy for me to know if a client really rocks with me because most pay more than I'm actually charging and not to mention send people my way. That's how I know they really, really appreciate what I do. That it's more than just a haircut.

CHAPTER SEVEN:
SWEEP UP THE HAIR

In a literal sense, sweeping up the hair means just that. Collecting all of the hair from the floor after a haircut is vital to keeping the barbershop clean and sanitary. I've worked with barbers who allow literal chunks and piles of hair to lay all over the floor for hours before they tend to it. Not only is that unprofessional, but it is also unsanitary. What I've learned from various past experiences is that those who usually leave clutter on the floor, their lifestyles generally match that same exact clutter. More often than not, their whole life models that same dysfunction. Meaning, their life is in disarray and often they find themselves in toxic relationships, friendships, and situations. There's usually not a lot of organization in their life, not because they're bad people but mainly because they've never decluttered. There's clutter in their life simply because what's been cut away has never been discarded. I've picked up on things like that just by working with different types of barbers. Different ethnicities and genders but all the same clutter. You can usually tell how they flow and how they approach life or even their goals based on their sense of organization. Failure to maintain a clean station is symbolic of an untidy lifestyle. I know this may sound a bit much, but any barber that has been cutting for 10 plus years, especially in different working environments can attest to similar habits of bad barbering. It's very important to regularly do a deep cleaning not only within the shop but internally as well. Focus your time and energy on proper mental health. When your mentals are aligned, everything else seems to fall right in place. Clutter has a tendency to be a thief of potential momentum. Try your best to handle things as they come, instead of pushing things to the side without addressing them. If not, the accumulation of clutter will soon follow. I'm not saying on rare occasions that things don't come up which prevent a prompt cleaning due to heavy work flow. However, if time is spent properly, the sweep up or cleanup will become more second nature. Without even focusing on it, attention to detail will become part of your daily routine. Barbershops by nature have a lot of traffic but the chairs are what require specific attention. Wiping down the chair and properly disinfecting everything speaks a lot about the character of a barber and how they approach their profession. It also speaks of consideration for the public as a whole.

With hair specifically, there's a lot of DNA found inside. You don't just leave that laying around for folk to track around. It gets tracked in people's cars as well as their homes or wherever it is that they go. Who really wants a part of themselves shared with others without their knowledge or consent? Well, that's what happens when barbers fail to properly dispose of their client's hair. Hair on the floor isn't just a chapter title, it also specifically speaks to overall neglect. I myself have been guilty of this behavior. When you first come into the industry, a lot more is learned on the floor that was never taught in barber school. All the experiences both good and bad are what ultimately build the overall character and skill set of a well-rounded master barber. I'm not suggesting that the academies don't do a good enough job teaching the trade, there's just something different about cutting hair under pressure as a rookie without any true experience in a Licensed Barbershop. In order to become a Diamond, the Charcoal must first withstand a tremendous amount of pressure. Followed by an excruciating amount of heat. The final step of the process is the cut.

Sweeping up the hair in a non-literal sense also pertains to the overall personal environment of the shop. We've got to sweep out the bad in order to maintain the professionalism and quality of a well-balanced and healthy barbershop. It is important that every shop do a thorough deep cleaning from time to time. Both on the shop itself and specifically, the barbers. A good haircutter does not mean a good barber. In order to have a prosperous shop, all barbers must have a mutual understanding of customer service, sanitation, and proper hair care. As I mentioned before, hair is very powerful. Even if we go all the way back to biblical times and focus our attention on a mighty warrior named Samson. In the Bible, Samson was one of the strongest men that has ever lived. However, he was naive to the cunningness of a beautiful woman named Delilah and had his power and strength stripped from him during a haircut. Samson's strength wasn't in his triceps nor his biceps but instead, it was embedded in his hair follicles. When his enemies discovered the secret of his strength being related to his hair, they sent Delilah to cut his hair while he was sleeping. To their own demise, they didn't destroy his hair follicles, so his hair grew back and so did his power. Samson was able to take down his enemies with the power that God gave him which was symbolic of his locks. If they really wanted to stop him, they would have cut off his head after they shaved his head but instead, they stripped him of his eyesight. Completely blind, he regained his strength and destroyed an army. I say it again, there is power in your hair, even more so, there's power in the Almighty God.

As early as 1619 when African Slaves were brought to the Jamestown Colony, one of the first orders of business was to cut off their locks and braids. They were stripped of any potential resemblance to where they came from. I believe the goal was to completely change their appearance to look less of who they were initially created to be. With the intention of restructuring their entire being. Without any regard, part of their power was taken away which connected them back to their roots. Kind of similar to military boot camp, but instead slavery was ten times more brutal. However, the goal is still the same, off with the old and in with the new. Before the time of slavery, we have the example of

Samson. Without question, there's a true significance to the cutting of hair. So in connection to the barbershop, you don't want to undermine the importance and symbolic value of what hair really is. Chris Rock even made a movie about the symbolism of hair. He titled it "Good Hair." I mean, not to sound cliché but hair is an entity all by itself. In a cultural sense, if a lion didn't have his mane, he wouldn't be quite complete. He definitely wouldn't look like the king of the jungle. It's more than just a look, hair connects many generations. It's also more than just a clump of clutter on the floor, it's the first thing that people see when they look at you. Hair can be whatever you want it to be, as long as it's not cluttered on the floor. Sweep up the hair from the floor.

The main issues that I've seen in barbershops are people who completely disregard space as a whole. So if you're letting clutter pile up, it's not only in your workspace but it's flowing over into other work areas. Believe it or not, this type of behavior can be contagious. Without even being aware, you can adopt the bad habits of fellow barbers. Habits that are detrimental to potential career growth and opportunity. We've all heard it said, "You are what you eat", although that holds true I'd also like to reiterate, "You are who you surround yourself with". Show me a man's circle and I'll show you his potential. People either inspire you or drain you, so be selective of the company that you keep. Bad habits can become your habits just by association. For instance, the capes that we put around people and potentially, different amounts of foreign hair attached to them if we don't disinfect them. Barbers continually drape people's necks, if we don't take these capes to the dry cleaners and get them properly cleaned, that's a whole new level of unsanitary. You don't want past hair of 10 clients ago stuck on you. If it's around the inside of the cape, it's now on your neck and falling down your back holding firmly to your shirt. Imagine that somebody's hair is on you with a potential scalp condition. This may or may not be harmful but to gamble the odds are just inconsiderate of the overall public. Neck strips, clean capes, and disinfects are key essentials to avoiding the transfer of potentially, harmful bacteria. Bacteria is literally everywhere but the invasion of bad bacteria can have negative effects on the immune system. We need good bacteria to help fight off foreign pathogens that can cause infection and other health problems.

People don't think that it can go that deep, but it very well does go that deep. Hair carries a lot. So it's not so much being an eyesore on a floor in the barbershop, it's the proper sanitation that comes along with the entire process of proper barbering. Rather it's with the capes, tools, or work area you don't want to just leave it. You've got to discard it, you've got to brush it off the tools and spray those babies down. You've got to rotate clean capes as well as wipe the hair off the seat of the chair with disinfectant wipes. At the end of the workday, when you don't sweep and mop the floor, hair travels literally everywhere.

When I moved out of my first house before I got married, I never realized just how much hair I had cut in my home until I was packing up. I didn't even realize how far these hair strains were traveling. It stuck out specifically when I cleaned my kitchen, I got all the dishes out of my dish drainer, and when I lifted the rack up, there was a few tiny pieces of hair in the bottom tray of the dish drainer in my kitchen. Ironically, my kitchen wasn't even near my living room where I was cutting hair. Say this with me "hair travels everywhere". You have to be mindful of that kind of stuff. And if you're not paying attention to it, I mean, Lord only knows how far you can go with disinfecting a client. Silly me, I was a poor college student in desperate need of cash, so I turned my place into an illegitimate barbershop. Not a business nor personal license in sight, I cut hair around the clock. I've literally cut hair at all hours of the day and night, just doing anything to try and get some traction. Your local neighborhood 24hour Barber. Another thing that hurt me drastically is the fact that I never applied a convenience fee to any of my clients. Most of which at the time were very close friends. Back then, I didn't want to lose them as clients. I didn't see it the other way around, which is they'd be losing a very clean, convenient, and cost effective personal barber! I never charged for fuel as I traveled from house to apartment to trailer, etc. I never charged for not only bringing the barbershop experience to the client without a wait time but cleaning up any trace that I was ever there. As for "Sweeping Up The Hair", let's just say that I've done my fair share. Just simply put, I did what I thought I had to do. I was young and professionally inexperienced but, I was hungry. As a result, I never saw the true value in the services that I provided. I mean man, I was "Uber Cuts" well over a decade before the concept of Ubering ever existed. I have several dozen witnesses who can attest to that. Needless to say, I shot myself in the foot big time monetarily. It truly amazes me the amount of money these convenience based businesses are generating in this day and time. It's absolutely unreal the amount of money that people will pay these days just to not have to be inconvenienced. I was extremely naive and had no clue that I was "Mr. Convenience," but I bet the people I was cutting did. Especially considering there was literally one urban shop in town with only 2 chairs within a 25mile radius. I was solely focused on building at whatever cost. It took a lot more to be a Barber back then. There were no local Academies or examples of what real master barbering look liked. The closest is in Knoxville Tennessee, about an hour and a half away. Definitely not a sought after trade in my hometown, especially during the 80's, 90's, and early 2000's. I don't in any way suggest that anyone gets their experience this way because I completely devalued the proper training needed to be a true craftsman. Not to mention I had random peoples' hairs in every corner of my house. Don't get me wrong, I ran the vacuum and cleaned my home regularly, but hair travels in places that you can't see. At that time, I was completely oblivious to my lack of proper hair care. But more importantly to leave the hair cutting in the shop and preserve my home for peace and relaxation. Early on in my career, I never saw it necessary to show the public the importance of respecting personal space. Trust me when I say, there is value in finding a place to disconnect from all the noise. It's healthy to dwell in that place as often as possible. Wherever that may be, obviously that looks differently for different people.

That's something within the boundaries of customer service that can also run off the clientele. Not just dirty clippers, but dirty capes can cause ringworm, which can lead to medication and doctor visits. I mean, all that stuff adds up. Hair on the floor, you don't want to just disregard or leave it. Please have attention to detail and take proper care of it because it's not just a simple thing. It's not just a small follicle. It is powerful and it's not to be left unattended.

Personally, I do my best to clean up behind every client. Sometimes in high peak seasons, for instance, Christmas, Thanksgiving, and Easter, if you're just doing one after another, it's hard to get every chunk. I try and stay mindful though to set the tone for the shop as a whole. Not just to set an example for the barbers but I don't want a client to come to the chair stepping on hair that's not theirs. So for me personally, I have something called an EYE-VAC system which I use in all my locations. It makes clean up so much more convenient. All you have to do is kick it with your foot and it sucks up clumps of hair along with neck strips. This system saves on your back since you don't have to bend down with the traditional dustpan and manually sweep up the hair. I put this device at every station so that no barber has a chance to allow clutter to overtake the shop.

Once it accumulates in the EYE-VAC system it's a lot easier to disregard at the end of the work day. By simply detaching the base of the system and pouring out the collected hair and reattaching the base, each barber becomes more efficient. These efforts keep us right back in the loop with taking care of the customers and not spending as much time on the cleanup.

I now have several broom boys. This all happened by default. My little cousin, Marquis Ballenger, propositioned me for working off his haircut when I very first opened my barbershop. Considering I was a one-man show when I initially opened, I kind of needed someone to sweep up and answer the phone so that I could focus on the actual haircut. Quis, saw an opportunity to get a free haircut which turned into a part-time job at the age of 11 years old. I was supposed to have some barbers come in by opening day, but they lagged behind in school. So, my first six months in business, I was a one man show. Ironically, my little cousin comes by to get a haircut and says, "Cuz, if you'll pay me a few dollars for sweeping my hair up, man, I can get me some McDonald's across the street?" And I thought, man, that's dope that my cousin had that grind in him. 10, 11 years old, he's thinking about how to eat, literally. He could have just thought to ask me for the money but instead, he chose to work for it. But I loved it, man. So I gave him five bucks. He lit up like a Christmas Tree, "Man, for real?" Then he said, "Can I come back tomorrow?" So instead of him catching the school bus home, he'd come straight to the barbershop after school and all day on Saturdays. I taught him not only the importance of keeping hair off the floor but also the value of hard work.

Some days, I'd say to myself "Man, what have I started". But in all, it was a beautiful thing to experience because not only did he keep coming back, he beat me there on the weekends. Even in the summertime when he would be out of school, this dude would have his grandmother drop him off in front of the shop with a cup of coffee and a McDonald's biscuit. In my head, I can still see him sitting in the parking lot waiting for me to pull up. And as soon as we unlock the door, he gets his broom, his bleach, his mop and he starts going to town. We worked out an arrangement for a weekly payment system. He felt like a grown up going to the Mall on Saturday nights after closing the shop. He had saved the money that he earned through the week so that he could splurge at the Mall. He'd meet up with his buddies from school but the only difference was that he had a job and money in his pockets that he had earned by working.

The other kids his age started seeing that Marquis is in middle school like them and he's got a job, and they started kind of gravitating to us. I made him some business cards. He felt like a big shot man. If you're in the sixth grade with a job and a business card, you're in a whole different stratosphere. I did my best to teach him the value of a dollar. How to properly save his money.

It's refreshing for me to have witnessed his work ethic at such a young age because I feel like a lot of kids nowadays are so glued to technology and don't have any get up and go about themselves. It isn't like when we were kids, you couldn't just sit around in the house, you had to go out and play or do something. Be home when that street lights come on though. But that's not their story. That's not their generation. Their path is a little bit more technologically driven. Modern day game systems are so advanced with graphics and storylines that they literally suck you into another world. If my generation had access to the same technology at such a young age, we'd probably be equally enthused.

When my generation becomes senior citizens and we can't take care of ourselves, we'd better hope we've done everything possible to assist the next generation. Helping them get equipped at a young age to declutter, and "Sweep up the hair from the floor." It's going to be the young people that are running the world someday. If they aren't equipped, I'm afraid we are in bad shape. I'm ashamed to say that before I started doing this mentee program, I didn't really have much faith in the next generation. Even seeing different families coming into the barbershop and how drastically different modern day parenting is. I'm blessed to say that by seeing the growth of a few young ins like my little cousin Marquis and the challenges that he had to face as a kid, anything is possible for anyone regardless of age who dares to dream.

I'm grateful to say that all is not lost. There's still a good number of people out there who like myself do not shy away from hard work and embrace life's challenges head-on. Every apprentice who's ever worked at TaylorMade has learned proper sweeping and disposing of the hair, cleaning, and answering the phone. If they are willing to do that at such a young age, what can't they do by the time they're 18, 21, 30, and so on and so forth. I really do believe for them that the sky's the limit. The Taylor Made brand is not just about haircuts, it's about the community as a whole. This concept of mentorship wasn't something that I personally intended to do, it was just something that was pulled out of me by my little cousin trying to get a Big Mac and French Fry. Nonetheless, I am forever grateful for the experiences and all life's lessons along the way. This thing called success isn't a destination, it's more like a journey. There's so much to be said about the journey, all the highs and lows are what create the learning curve along the way. So much can come from life's lessons while climbing the ladder of success.

Philanthropy Work

Even outside the mentorship program, we've not only mentored young men, but we've also had a few young ladies as well. Both of our receptionists Camesha Stevens & Rochelle Fisher have done a tremendous job assisting with this. The young ladies don't do too much of the manual labor, they just mainly stay behind the receptionist's desk, answering the phone and signing people in. We want young men to realize the importance of doing manly deeds. Outside of the mentee program, we also do an annual scholarship for graduating high school seniors going to college. We also have a scholarship with both East Tennessee State University and Tusculum University. Both of our locations are neighbors to these institutions so it only made sense to partner with them. We have our annual back to school community bash every July, the weekend before school starts back. This event includes free book bags, school supplies, haircuts, food, games, and more.

At our most recent event, we gave away 415 bags stuffed with school supplies. We fed over 300 people and cut over 100 people. We had a gentleman who came from a real estate company and gave away cash to kids who answered trivia questions based on credit scores. The local barber academy gave away a full 20K scholarship to a barber school. That was really dope, much love to Crown Cuts Academy for doing that. During Thanksgiving, we partner with a company called Big Boys LLC, and we sponsor 50 pre-boxes, turkeys, stove top stuff, three vegetables, and a dessert with rolls. We not only deliver them to you, but if you are completely without shelter or have no means to prepare the food, we cook it and bring it to you ready to serve.

Christmas time, we do stuff trees in both locations with unlimited pre-wrapped gifts for kids K through eighth grade. Anytime you come into the shop from December the first to December the 31st, you can get a gift from under the tree. We've even got jazzy in the past few years, and instead of a traditional candy cane, we try to find the Skittle flavored or the Oreo flavored. We do our best to add a little to your holiday. At the beginning of every semester, we set up our mobile unit on E.T.S.U. And Tusculum campus and give free haircuts to students. Giving them a fresh look to start the semester.

These are a few things that we've kind of indulged in that go beyond the "haircut." The journey has been one of the most fulfilling and refreshing things I've ever experienced. Something so simple as a small gesture and how far it can go. Seeing a single mother, maybe 25 at most with four kids, no father in sight come to our back to school bash and say, "We have no food to eat tonight nor any money for book bags of school supplies." and how much she appreciated the assistance means everything. Defiantly makes the process of putting everything together worthwhile. Now we have companies wanting to partner for next year to contribute shoes. So we can not only do shoes, we can even potentially have clothes going forward. This thing can get ridiculously big, man. It can go so far beyond TaylorMade if I can get other businesses around me to see the value in partnering up and putting our finances together and the magic that can come from our overall collective effort. Instead of making it a July thing or a before school starts thing, we could even do a quarterly event, four times a year all sponsored by local businesses.

Once I got started with that, it opened me up to various possibilities and the potential of literally anything. Not allowing myself to be put in a place to think that nothing is possible because I'm seeing too much manifestation. Not so much for me and my business and my family, but just seeing how many people are blessed by these efforts. One thing that I do want to touch on briefly that I'm not really okay with is the overall community "pat on the back". Over the years, I've heard a lot of "I'm proud of you bro, glad to see somebody doing something around here." I hate when I hear statements like that because truth be told, I'm just doing my part. I'm not doing anything special, I'm just doing my job. And if everybody did their job, nobody would stand out. So don't pat me on the back nor salute or congratulate me. Help me, partner with me, team up with me if you share the same sentiments as I do for the community, and let's do more together as a unit.

But I think it's almost a cop out to say, "Man, I respect you and look up to you and believe in what you're doing and keep doing what you're doing, keep going man, the community needs it." Well, dang, if you feel that the community needs more effort, why aren't you doing anything about that? Why aren't you personally giving more effort and helping the overall growth of the people? I keep my head up with my chest out and just do my best to do what I can. But I mean, we all have a job to do. Regardless of how much of an impact you think you may or may not have if everybody pitched in and did something I believe the odds would be endless. It takes no effort to clap from the sideline, but it takes a lot of sweat equity to do your personal part in making the community a better place. Small efforts become significant efforts over time. In the same regard, a group effort can have a monumental impact overall. There is really strength in numbers. Our lives are not comic books, Superman isn't gonna show up at the perfect time of crisis and save us from trouble. Say this with me, "There is no such thing as a Super hero". And if there was, that's entirely too much responsibility to throw off on one individual. If the hero dies, then what's the plan, are we all doomed? Let's stop looking to be saved and start doing a little saving of our own. It's our own civic duty to do what we can to add value to our local communities. Selflessness will eventually lead us all into the Promised Land. Honestly, it wouldn't take much, just one simple kind gesture at a time. Together, we can all do our part and keep the "Hair Off The Floor".

CHAPTER EIGHT:
BEHIND THE CHAIR OF MY FAITH

I cherish the truth. I tell things the way that I see them. The truth is that I'm not a great barber. My clients will tell you otherwise, but I know for a fact that my talent to produce nice haircuts is a gift from up above. Before I learned how to cut hair, I first discovered an interest in art. As a young kid from first to second grade, I could do sketches that could almost match the level of a typical 15-16yr old-year. This uniqueness earned me the attention of a few art academies that wanted me to be part of their programs. I was so young, I didn't quite know what I wanted to do with my life. One thing I do know is that I wasn't really motivated by the thought of staring at an easel for hours trying to create a masterpiece. Although I feel like art was without question a gift, I honestly didn't see it as a passion but instead more of an escape. A way to break away from reality from time to time. I've never got the same response from a sketch or painting as I did from a well-tailored Haircut. Once I hit sixteen and felt more comfortable using the Clippers and Trimmers, it became more about making my clients feel good about the cut that I just gave them. Boosting their confidence as well as their self-worth. Once I get that classic reaction when I hand over the mirror, mixed with a million-dollar smile; that's the confirmation before the actual payment transaction. That's an unspoken understanding between the barber and the client that all expectations have been exceeded. And that feeling ladies and gentlemen is absolutely priceless. Being able to add a bit a value to people's day is a distinct privilege that barbers have. In my younger days I became addicted to the process of Barbering. The feeling of exchanging good energy. Something that started off as a hobby but quickly grew into a passion. A passion that still allows me to express myself artistically to this very day. Over the years I've cut hundreds of logos, free hand designs, three dimensional designs and more. I must say that I get excited the most when a client comes in with a concept of a cool design. When I'm allowed free reign to do abstract art in the haircut, I almost feel like a kid again. Those specific haircuts without question take me back to the days of sketches in downtime way back in elementary school. It's sort of like a natural high. That's when I feel like I'm most in my element. When people operate in their element, they're most likely to succeed at whatever it is that they're doing. That's not an opinion, that's a fact. The reason being is, the person is then operating in their gift. Gifts are God given; they're not worked for nor earned. Simply a gift from up above and every single soul on this earth has a gift to some degree. The sad part is that most folk die without ever know exactly what that gift is or how it feels to live life thriving in your specific lane. Whatever your gift is, never be a lane watcher. Instead focus all your energy and strengths on being that absolute best at whatever it is you are called to do. Barbering is undoubtedly an art form, an art that has been around since the times of ancient Egypt. God gifted me with the ability of art, for that I am forever grateful. First and foremost, respectfully I am an Artist.

Through my gift, God has opened so many doors. It is beyond words how things and uncommon favor can open up for you when you fully embrace your God given abilities. These opportunities have allowed me to see that barbering can be a vehicle that can completely surpasses an individual haircut. A vehicle that has many lanes as well as a wide verity of potential. This potential however doesn't come readily available without much personal sacrifice and dedication. It's not enough just to have the ability, the trade must be worked. Different levels within the trade require a different amount of focus and attention. For years I never saw past the beginning stages for master barbering, which is chair rental. In some cases, chair rental can be very profitable depending on the barber/stylist and their specific approach to the craft. Everyone's career is different. Time and proper money management play a major part in this process. Nothing is given, everything is earned. So you see, it's not enough to be gifted, if the individual does nothing with the gift. Faith without works is completely dead. That is not an opinion but instead comes directly from the good book. Trust fully in the one who gifted you and you can accomplish literally anything. These accomplishments will be the product of faith as well as some sweat equity.

I will reach every destination by faith, wherever God needs me to go through barbering, but the haircutting profession itself must not be my main focus. My main objective must be eternal life with Christ Jesus. Nothing here on earth is permanent or meant to last. Everything is borrowed time and possession. Contrary to what most people believe, my business nor my brand belong to me. It all belongs to God, TaylorMade was uniquely crafted and designed by him. I still remember the day and where I was when the concept became so clear to me. I was at my apartment in Campus Ridge right behind East Tennessee State University, sitting on my back deck with my boy Earnest Weaver from Miami Fl. I was talking about how my clientele had grown to a place I never imagined. How mind blowing but at the same time authentic. Before I could finish talking, he says, "Bruh, that's because you're Tailor-Made, from the ground up!" Then he chuckled and said yo, TaylorMade is the new movement. We both cracked up because the concept was so genuine. Definitely not another cookie cutter brand name. Not only is my last name Taylor but my journey has been undoubtedly "Tailor Made". Those who sincerely know me, know that everything in my life, I've gotten the hard way and can appreciate the authenticity of my brand. I was never given money nor any access to a network of individuals that can assist with my career. Being a young entrepreneur and feeling like I was finally starting to get some momentum was very exciting to say the least. I was still in college, not a barber license in site, but as soon as Miami said the word "Tailor Made," it felt like the missing piece to my barbering identity. I still get chills thinking about that moment because I knew then how to approach my entire branding concept and exactly how I wanted to go about it. Considering I was a Computer Graphic Design Major, I remember that night going to the computer lab and creating a personal business card with a pearl white background, I was dressed in a suit and shades complimented with a pair of chrome Andis Master Clippers with the word -TaylorMade Precision- alongside the image. Definitely not the best business card, but again everything in-house. Nothing given, everything was literally Tailored, I stand by that concept. Not just the means of having a job but also the effect that the brand could have overall. The amount of people potentially blessed by a simple concept of community. It was then that I felt the most purpose behind my passion.

Everything and everyone around me is created by God. My family and friends, everyone I've ever known have been handcrafted by the Almighty. My love and appreciation for art goes deeper than what an ordinary eye can see. I use to watch the famous artist, Bob Ross, on Television back in the day. I observed his skill with awe and was amazed with what he could accomplish with the mere stroke of a paintbrush. I was baffled over his calm poised demeanor and smooth tone of voice. He created masterpieces so effortlessly. That's the type of artist which I've aspired to be. One that can turn a blank canvas into a complete work of perfection. Who knew that a middle-aged white guy with a huge Afro, could capturing the attention of a young black kid in East Tennessee while painting on television. The most fascinating part was that these televisions shows where thirty minutes on average. So to see him work basically under a stop watch was the wow factor to me. The lesson then became, "Can You Produce Magic In Minutes."

I liked electronics as a kid, but sketches and drawings where my favorite pass time. I could sketch nonstop for hours and hours. Time was never a factor when I was in my element. If I was going through some tough times or I found myself in tight spots, I drew my pain out. Sometimes the sketches were dark, and other times they were more peaceful. One thing is for certain, whatever I was going through then in my life, my inner battles always came out in my artwork. All emotions between rage and peace came out in my work. I obviously didn't see that being the case at the time, I was way too young to comprehend what was happening. I do not believe that was intentional, however every artist has their own distinct way of conveying their art.

When I would draw, it was as if time stood still. Right from the time I got home from school until dinner time, I would be hard at it trying to produce something hot. I wouldn't realize that five hours had gone by already. Captivated by what I'm bringing from my mind into manifestation, I just got lost within the work. I felt as if I was the closest to God when I was in my zone, making use of the gift and abilities that he gave me. Have you ever done something so efficient but with ease to the point that it felt like breathing? Well, that is what art does for me. Although I've gone from sketches to haircuts, it's still all the same. Art is and forever will be a major part of my life.

I'm human, I can be going through a rough patch in my marriage or about to go in on my son, or even worse my coworkers are tripping, yet I would find comfort in my art. When I cut the clippers on, I always hear from God. Beneath the humming or noise around me I can still manage to hear his voice ringing out to me. He stands by me all the time and just like the air we breathe, I can't see him, but I know he is right there 24/7. Without a doubt, I feel that I could hear him talking to me through the process of the work that I'm doing. He calms me down and gets me back on track. He helps me to see the bigger picture. Like a whisper from a guardian angel, I will hear his voice saying calmly to me "It's about the journey, Micah Don't rush it".

Slow down and embrace the ride while I drive you to your destiny. Appreciate the process. If not, you're missing the whole point. Those soothing words are always energetic and invigorating. After that spiritual pep talk, a wave of comfort will wash over my body and soul. In that moment, I feel blessed to be a blessing. No longer focused on what didn't go right, but instead being grateful for what could've gone wrong. Redirecting my energy into a place of gratitude. Fact of the matter is, people aren't perfect so life will never be perfect. Situations and circumstances will arise however if we learn to turn our overall focus to the blessings in our lives and not the problems, I believe that to be an expression of appreciation to God. Appreciate him for what he's done in our lives and keeping us throughout the process. A process that at times seems to be too much weight for one person but he's never failed us. If we've managed to maintain good health, that is the greatest gift ever. The world will teach otherwise, but Health is Wealth. It's important that we're mindful of that truth.

It's not about how much you can accumulate in this life. If you turn on the TV for hours or watch the news or constantly browse social media, these things will train you to believe that you have to hoard your success so that you can flaunt it in people's faces. Wrong, there is more to life than the stuff we collect. In my opinion there is absolutely nothing wrong with working hard and enjoying some of the fruits of your labor. I'm not in any way implying that we can't or shouldn't enjoy nice things but if they become collector's items that mean more than life itself then it becomes all vanity. Life has a funny way of training us to believe that we're in some crazy competition. From early youth we're taught to be competitive in life. As Kids we have aspirations to have the Biggest House, Biggest Car and the Most money in the bank; instead of shelter, transportation, and our bills paid. As I mentioned, there's nothing wrong with nice things, but I do personally see something wrong in hoarding up the excess which could potentially be used to be a blessing to other people in various situations. Resources are meant to be shared. If you're a believer in the Almighty, then you know that he is more than resourceful. He has more than enough and has always been more than enough. It's not necessary for us to get caught up in society's views on success. If we're not careful, we'll never believe in enough or be grateful for what we have. I'm a true believer that we're blessed to be a blessing. And that our blessings where never intended to specifically bless just us. Luke 12:48 says, "To Whom Much Is Given, Much Will Be Required." So, if we've been given much; its only right that we carry on in that same act of giving. Both in our time, finances, and resources. Acknowledging that everything comes from God anyhow. Once we realize that, we understand that we don't gain anything from hoarding the blessing. I encourage anyone reading this book to be intentional on being a blessing to as many people as you can before you leave this earth. This world is overflowing with takers, be the exception to the rule and retire as a giver. You'll never have a lack in any area of your life, this I assure you.

I wouldn't consider myself a philanthropist. I simply consider myself a child of God. He first gave to me and told me to go this way. It's not as if I'm a good man with this huge heart. If good men are lined up for rewards or awards, I don't qualify to be in their league. I'm a sinner with sins that run deep and flaws that only God himself can perfect. I'm a human who makes mistakes each and every single day. So I don't want to portray the image of a saint which I'm not. I'm the lowest of the lows who has been barred underneath rock bottom. I'm just very grateful and fortunate to be saved by grace and God's endless mercies over my life. Just like many of the people in the Bible, I myself was a lost cause. I'm just thankful that God intentionally uses imperfect people to carry out his agenda. The good book is full of examples where he's used some of the worst people possible to do his work. And through that work, completely changing their lives. I am thankful that he doesn't expect us to have it all together. He meets us right where we're at and does what only he can do. Turning dirty lumpy pieces of coal into shiny Diamonds.

God reminds me of who He called me to be and what He has planned for me. I try to stay mindful of the bigger picture. Keeping my focus on what really matters and understanding that it's all by the power of God. His blessings are in abundance, too numerous to count and too large for one room to contain. His blessings are sufficient for everyone. He doesn't have to rob another man to bless Micah. My friend He doesn't have to cause an overdraft in your account to bless me, God has more than enough for us all. Once we fall in love with that concept, we don't see each other as competition. In fact, we eliminate the concept of competition, because if there was one; God himself has already been deemed the champion. I like to refer to him as the "Pound For Pound Heavy Weight Champion Of The Universe" He's never lost a fight!

He's got enough for whoever is in need. A lot of people don't see it like that because they lean on their own understanding. Believing in their own personal abilities instead of trusting in the most high. They think they can get to the top by stepping on the heads of other people. How cruel can we be to think that we have to use people in some twisted bubble of manipulation in order to advance in life. We are too carnally minded to understand that destroying someone else's life to save our own or planting seed of deception in someone else's business to make ours flourish doesn't make us smart but instead foolish. That's not how it works. In fact, that type of behavior only sows seed toward our own demise. Creating room in your life for more discord and dysfunction. So be part of someone else's success story. We gain absolutely nothing from trying to be a hindrance to another person's growth. In fact, in only makes sense to align yourself with people being blessed. Perhaps you'll be next in line for a blessing. One thing is for certain, blessings never flow from malicious intent. So be a leg up for someone you know. Be a helping hand and support people along the way. Never be a person who covets the blessings of other people. We should all applaud and celebrate victories. Even if they're not our own.

For you reading this book, I have a little advice that I'd like to share with you. If you take heed to His voice and listen to God's plans, you will enjoy his infinite grace. His grace you don't even have to work for or rob Peter to pay Paul. God's unmerited favor. Don't make plans or decisions for yourself without consulting him first, stay in your lane. Don't jump when you get frustrated or you are fed up with life. Only jump when he says. "All right. Now it's time to go." Let him be the director of your symphony. You just play your part, then use the gift that He given you to bless humanity and to proclaim his Word. Sharing the gospel also known as "The Good News" with as many people as possible. Be a light in a world that seems to be darker than ever. A world that needs a glimpse of hope and possibility. Now more than ever we not only need love, but we also need Jesus. He's the only answer that can solve such a crazy problem. His ways are higher than our own and if we lean on him and trust his judgment, we never lose. So, share Hope instead of Hate.

I don't believe in exceptional people. What I do believe is that everybody has a gift, talent or innate ability. Nobody born of a man and a woman is a mistake, period. Each person's birth is purposeful, meaningful and significant in the eyes of God. He does not create any human being empty without a gift or talent. Your existence is purposeful. With that purpose comes some form of a gift. The majority of people who are not successful are those who have not yet tapped into their gifts. I try my best to be available, especially for younger barbers who ask questions. Note, I don't push faith on people, but if they open that door, I try to kick it off the hinges. Sharing my faith and belief, I use that opportunity to minister to them and encourage them with love. The last thing you need when you are longing for something that money can't buy is to be ran over like a Mack truck. Don't over complicate the gospel. It's not our job as believers to convert people, just share the good news. So by all means don't be a bible basher. We as people should never make it hard for non-believers to come to Christ, especially if Christ himself never made it that way. We should follow the standard and lead with love, leaving judgment out of the equation. No other religion in the world offers a savior which dies for Us. That should be so encouraging today that there's hope for tomorrow.

I'd never want an individual to feel like I'm forcing religion on them because it wasn't forced on me. Salvation was an open invitation for me. God created us with the intelligence to think and make decisions for ourselves. Without pause, I know what God has done for me and the plans he has in store for me. The plans include my prosperity. With God, I'm safe and cannot be hurt. Through my gift, I feel absolutely alive. Outside of that would be prayer time. I feel him in a different way when I pray. God has a unique way of revealing himself to us in various ways.

Spending time with God is imperative, I don't joke with my quiet time. I can concentrate better on my prayers around the period when my surrounding is quiet, with no distractions or diversions. Taking time to truly embrace moments in his presence. Knowing that there's no better place to be. Spending time with someone who's love is not conditionally based. As humans we often times fluctuate with love. God never wavers, he's loved us before time ever existed.

So we can find comfort in loving him, because he first loved us. That's a love that will forever stand the test of time. Some refer to it as Perfect Love.

I observed something about hearing from God directly when I'm praying. He uses a different voice. It is almost quieter as if he's louder when I'm in my zone. It's like I can see the clearer direction or hear clearer instructions. Only prayer time can bring you truly close to God because that's when you can hear his voice better. It's important that we get proper instruction for the journey. A journey that sometimes can get pretty intense. No matter the storm, as long as he's with us; the winds follow his command. There's real victory not only in his name's sake but having a relationship with him. Setting aside time to hear from him, knowing that his plans are to prosper his people. That should be encouraging news right there. The reassurance in knowing that despite the battle, the victory is already won. Look at David, a young undersized boy going against a Philistine Giant named Goliath. Clearly he didn't win this battle using brute strength, this battle was undoubtedly won by the power of the Almighty. Trusting in God's strength, timing and ability for your life, can be the difference between victory or defeat. A young boy that grew to be a King. Considering he was undersized the odds say he was clearly outmatched. Again as I mentioned before, trust in Gods strength, not your own.

I'm grateful for my blessings, although I'm undersized I've managed to overcome so many obstacles. I've heard every short joke known to man growing up. I've gotten the jokes about height my entire life. I'm 5'7" while all my closest homeboys were six foot plus. As kids and even now when we all get together, they still let me have it, "Sup, Lil man?" This of course is done with love, I've got nothing but love for my guys. However, the stature stigma still remains true. Most of the world equates overall greatness and potential with height and size. Being an "undersized" individual I find this rather amusing. I'm sure we can all look around and see tons of wasted stature running around here. That's if we're still suggesting that size is the advantage. I'm blessed to say that I wake up daily and defy those odds on a regular basis. My stature has never kept me from exceeding challenges in life. That's not to say that I haven't lost a few fights, buts it's not how hard you get hit but if you keep moving forward.

I'm putting my minimal height into maximum use. Do you know what they say about making lemonade out of the very lemons that life throws at you? That's what I'm doing. This specific batch just so happens to be Taylor-Made Lemonade, it's pretty sweet too. Other people who like myself are vertically challenged may have automatically discredited themselves, wallowing in their own disbelief because of someone else's belief. I don't allow people's opinions to outweigh my internal belief or divert my energy into something unproductive. I've used every foot and inch to bless humanity. What if I tell you that from a business perspective that I've accomplished more than many of my, tall friends? That's not bragging nor am I taking jabs but it's the truth. I say all this to say, never let anyone's opinion of you determine how you view yourself or how you approach life. I'm blesses to have friends who are like myself hard working and accomplished, we've all had jobs since the age of 15yrs old. None of us had an easy route into adulthood. Everyone has advantages and disadvantages, learn yours and get to work on your dreams regardless of circumstance. Play the cards that you are dealt. Never allow life to determine your limits. You have unlimited potential if you just believe.

I know for a fact that my friends don't mean any harm by calling me, "lil man", but it's almost like an unspoken rule in the world that says if you're undersized or even worse overweight, you're ruled out. You're not fit to run the race of life or you're not fit to fight the good fight. That's a fallacy and I'm living proof. I challenge anyone ready this book to take a brief self-examination. Realize your strengths as well as your weaknesses but don't be defined by either. If you're going to accomplish anything significant in life, it will not be by your own merit. Your size, ethnicity nor gender will be the thing that wills you into greatness. If by chance you become an exceptional human being, its simply because that's how God chose to write your story. He loves using individuals who are the most unqualified. His word is full of examples of people who did not qualify for the job.

God sends his precious angels to watch over us. They're always by our side every single step of the way. So, it's not by our power, might, height or size that anything good has gone our way. Giant or midget, it doesn't matter in the battles and the race of life. We are all created equal before God. That is why the Bible says that God is no respecter of persons. People can't take credit for the supernatural.

Faith

I encountered the Lord as a kid. God chose to use my grandmother to lead me to him. She was very dear to my heart. Her name was Mary Louise Goodman. She's deceased now. Her upbringing was very distorted, but her mother, my great-grandmother, was also a woman of Faith. All of my great grandmother's children, grand and great-grands know the word. They made sure of that. Even those who've gone astray, they know that word. That's just how my family is. It was never an option, but more so a way of life.

When I was with my grandmother, she taught me the power of prayer and how to fall in love with it. She prayed several times a day, so you could say it was in the bloodline. Everybody was introduced to God but some strayed. The sad thing is that I was one of those who fell into mischief myself which puts me into the category of the strayed ones. Even today, I'm not perfect. I have many flaws but I'm grateful that God sees me as a work in progress. The only person capable of reaching perfection is Jesus Christ himself.

I was taught the gospel in my early childhood. Those were the days when I was in the first grade and was going on trips with her. We would attend conferences with worldwide evangelists. I can remember being in the fourth grade at a conference in San Diego, California. A minister named Morris Cerullo came to preach that day. He had a worldwide outreach as well as some evangelists present at the event available for prayer. People queued before the minister to receive prayers. I and my grandmother fell in line to be prayed for too. When we got near she held my hands and two gentlemen prayed for us. All of a sudden something strange happened that I still find amazing to today. For whatever reason, the next thing I knew five people came around me. When they prayed for me, their voices were loud and radical. It was like they are crying desperately to God on my behalf. Those people were everywhere. They kept crying in prayer. "This one here. This one here is special. This one here is going to be a great leader for God." I was thinking within myself. "Who the heck are they talking about? I'm no leader, I'm nobody. I'm the kid that is considered "corny" at school. I'm the kid that comes from a middle-class family. I'm the kid that has little athletic ability. I'm the kid that doesn't get picked for the pickup game. I'm the kid with zero confidence in my ability to be great at anything other than drawing. Who are they talking about, man? Not me."

My grandmother saw everything, that day she witnessed to me that my calling was in ministry. God has revealed to me thru barbering that I'm in my ministry right now as we speak. I thought for years that this meant for literal, that I was supposed to pastor a church. However being called to minister doesn't necessarily mean from a pool pit inside the walls of a church. Ministry comes in many forms, and I consider myself bless to be called to minister to the community. I have a huge congregation. My chair is my ministry. I'm closer to my clients when they're in my chair than my pastor is to me when I'm in church. The only thing left would be to have the title "pastor". Which is something not to be taken lightly. I don't have a physical church. My main church is my barbershop and my congregation are my clients and the local communities. I wish my grandmother was still alive to see a glimpse of what God has been doing through me. She would then understand what the prayer time inside that conference years ago was about. To me, it was about this specific season that I'm living in. The prophecy of that year has come to pass. All Glory to God Almighty!

I feel like God has spoken to me clearly. What I'm doing now with my team for the children in this community is a testament that the work of my ministry has begun. We're rolling in the ministry as we speak. My ministry is beyond cutting hair. The shop stands as a prototype of my church. The haircut is the basic tool, and the vehicle that will drive us to where we are meant to be. I am forever grateful that he has allowed me to see the barbershop for so much more than grooming purposes. The shop is a safe haven for the community. Definitely a special place.

Earlier, I mentioned that after my grandmother brought up her children in the ways of the Lord years ago, I was among those who strayed. The gospel stayed inside me as a kid but as I grew older and entered my teenage years, I became wild. I strayed with the capital letter "S". I did a lot of outlandish things as most youngsters do out of curiosity. I was trying to experience the world. I wanted to see what life was all about. What's all this hype supposed to be about?

No matter how hard parents try to keep the feet of their kids on the right path, the world outside the walls of the home is equally powerful enough to pull them astray. But even as far away as I stayed, I always knew what was real. I've been in some very dark situations. I've even seen with my very own eyes demons, but I felt the presence of God with me even then. Although I could see the devil and his crew, God was with me there. Even when I was drunk or was at a party doing crazy things, he never left me. He hasn't left me yet. When I was out of my element and I moved away completely from him, he's still with me. He has always been the most consistent thing in my life. I'm forever grateful that he pulled me out of a dark pit and gave me a sense of purpose in life.

My faith plays a huge part in my profession. Barbers are not ordinary people like society leads us to believe. We don't just cut hair, we're actually more like therapists and counselors than grooming specialist. You can't effectively counsel somebody if you can't relate to what they're going through. If you haven't been to the bottom of life where they have been, you can't have the moral or psychological justification to advise them. If you're not experienced in dysfunction yourself, you can't speak from a genuine perspective. That's not to say that you can't offer a word of encouragement, but you certainly cannot relate. If I grew up with a silver spoon in my mouth and everything handed to me on a platter, how do I comprehend levels of poverty. If I have the finances to provide for myself and my life is on a roller coaster of wealth, how can I effectively sympathize much less counsel somebody going through a pit of financial hell? Unless I can speak from my own experiences in that same pit.

I believe that's what makes my situation genuine and effective. I'm not speaking from a place of optimism and love but a place of familiarity. If you're already going through hell, the keyword is for you to "Go Through". Don't stop. That is what I always do and that is why I used the word "familiarity". It's healthy when people look at me and the light bulb goes off in their heads. "Man, this dude, he's right. I grew up with him. I've seen his journey. He isn't just saying it. I've watched it. So I know he isn't just blowing smoke up my butt. I know he cares for me and he can relate to me. And if he can do it, if God can use him and he can overcome all sorts of challenges stuff, then I can too."

Life goes on. Don't forget that the only thing that is constant in life is change. Nothing stays the same, but having faith in God can change your circumstances completely. In my own words, I will say that faith is knowing how things turn out before you even get started. Faith is believing that things are going to work in your favor without knowing how hard the challenges will be or how difficult the tasks may be. You will be convinced in your heart that whatever is ahead is a done deal. Faith doesn't cause panic but assurance in God. His plan for your life is to prosper you.

Jeremiah 29:11 - For I know the plans I have for you, declares the Lord. Plans to prosper you and not to harm you, plans to give you hope and a future.

CHAPTER NINE:
CLIENTELE

As a young barber coming out of school, it was difficult to build a clientele. Fresh out of the Academy I started cutting in a town that wasn't my own. 806 East Center St. Kingsport Tn, right in front of Dale Street and right behind Lee Apartment Project Housing. Having to earn every individual that sat in my chair definitely made me into the barber that I am today. Again, prior to going to school, I had been cutting hair for 10yrs. This helped me with sharpening my cuts but I still had a lot to learn considering I'd never had any "shop" experience. The only advantage was that I had been cutting for all those years before going to barbering school. My cuts were up to par but my overall barbershop etiquette needed some developing. The lesson here is that Cutting Hair and Barbering are not the same. Thankfully, I had some loyal clients that didn't mind driving or I might have starved my first year in the game. Special shout out to Myreon, Chad, Whitt, Sanchez, Davy, Taylor, Love, Shakey, Frank, L.K., Smoke, Mouse, Ju, Rome, Squeek, D, Rahman. A few gentlemen throughout my career have been willing to commute regardless of location. Each barber in this industry needs people that they can count on, especially if the shop is unusually slow. As a teenager, I started cutting most of these guys for just $10. Fast forward 10yrs later and I'm a licensed professional in an actual business setting. I had taken the time to invest in my craft and although I still looked the same, I was a new person because I had credentials. The major difference forms an individual that has credentials and the one that does not is authorization. For instance, if I put on a police uniform with a badge, as well as place a light on the top of my car and ring a siren, I may have the look of the part. However, I haven't been given the right, authority, or credentials to make an arrest. In other words, I'd be unauthorized because I don't have the training and approval or backing of the jurisdiction. To make me an official member of the police force I would have to subject myself to the mandated training and prequalifying measures. The same is true with barbering. There is a lot that goes into the training required to be a Licensed Master Barber.

Clientele isn't indispensable, you can't just take it for granted. Networking is crucial, you must get out there and meet unfamiliar faces. You have to build and talk to people. You can't just sit in the shop marinating, waiting for somebody to walk up to you for a haircut. I've seen it happen on so many levels that it is just an epic failure. People may come in and they may come back to you and request you specifically. But nine times out of 10, that's not going to be what makes you successful. So, what I found in my journey to be most successful, as far as client retention, is giving away my product and time for free. Especially in the earlier stages of my career. I've probably given away more haircuts than I've actually sold, over the years. Say, for instance, you're in a food court at the mall and walk past an employee with a food tray from an eatery. This tray has free samples of some very appetizing food. You might not have been hungry but once you taste the product, you're more likely to buy a whole meal. As soon as the potential new client gets a sample of the product, it then becomes the barber's job to give them a proper service that warrants a consistent return. Repeat customers are earned, not given. Earning the business of new customers can be one of the industry's biggest challenges. All depends on the Barber and how they approach the craft. Some barbers are complacent and others are consistent with their energy. In order to fully maximize the license, the barber must learn to master the art of customer service as well as maintain a passion for the craft. It's not hard to tell who cuts strictly for income and who cuts for the love of the game.

If you order what you tasted for free and it's as good or even better than what you've tasted, now you're a customer. Now I have a taste for Charlies Steakery or Tokyo Express, whatever the case may be. So, literally for years, and even to this day, I go to the local Universities and I provide free haircuts in the spring and fall. I've heard it from younger barbers in the past, "You're a 20-year vet. You shouldn't have to do free cuts anymore." The misconception to that is the community aspect of barbering. It's not all about promoting and monetary gain. A fresh clean haircut can literally change someone's day. Why not use this craft to its full potential and build with the community as a whole? Connecting with people of all nationalities and offering a little encouragement with their cut. The chair can be therapeutic as well as refreshing. An experience that not a lot of industries offer. So if you look at it from a deeper perspective, sometimes the process; is the payment. There's no loss in giving the service away. Furthermore, there's no age limit to the grind. When signing up to take on the trade, in order to maximize the license's fullest potential the student must embrace the craft in its entirety. Shortcuts in any profession are a potential threat to progress and momentum. In order to master and craft, each level must be mastered from the bottom to the top. Nothing should be beneath the Barber. Community is essential to trade,

Every time we go out to the campuses our network increases on so many levels. Not only will they remember us, but in some cases, they may even recruit for us. So, when the students are walking around in the common areas with a fresh cut, it can be a conversation starter "Yo, where did you go to get that fresh haircut,", "Hey, my man, Micah Taylor hooked me up. He's not only cut me since I've been here but he's also been very consistent with cutting on campus. He's the only barber in the area that comes to us and gives away his services." Those things matter to not only a potential client but simply put another human being. So that's one thing I would challenge any younger barber to do, is to not look at how much you can get from your customers but rather how much are you willing to contribute to the craft. The industry as a whole goes as the barbers go. The process of schooling and learning each intricate part of the trade is important.

First, get as much repetition under your belt as possible. In order to be a polished barber, there needs to be at least a thousand plus haircuts under your belt. You can't come out with the hundred cuts thinking you've made it, you've arrived. In fact, you never arrive. I mentioned that in the past, it was a journey, it's not a destination. You never get there. For that very reason, continued education is very important. Every Barber/Stylist should attend yearly extended education. Remain a student throughout your career and you'll elevate to many different levels. Embrace the opportunity to learn new information and understand the fact that information changes situations. Applying new information to various seasons in life makes for an entire journey filled with potential.

Say this with me, Network, Network, Network. In everything you do, find a way to advertise your services. "Excuse me, sir, I see you already have a fresh haircut but if ever you're in need here's my card. Thank you for your time." This approach in no way discredits their current barber/stylist. Being respectful at the same time progressive with your marketing. Work up some kind of a deal if you have to. Twenty Five percent off when you bring in another customer. Half off if you bring in three people. Free cuts once a month for a whole year if you bring in twenty people. Barbers with no customers and no work ethic have a common saying, "The Shops have Been Slow". More often than not, it's the individual's efforts that are actually slow. World Wide, the Shop is the Shop, period! Different countries and different cultures, but the culture of a barbershop is the same whenever you go. Customers are earned, not given. You earn the right to change someone's appearance through your craft, that's a big deal. Unfortunately, not all barbers share those same sentiments. Complacency and entitlement run ramped in our industry. Sadly enough, there are those who look to be fed, instead of doing their own hunting. They don't see the thrill of the chase or the victory in the hunt. The Process.

Some folks are not willing to make those kinds of deals with the public for whatever reason. They think the public is supposed to guarantee them first. That's not a good way to build a foundation in barbering. I'd much rather be a barber with a third-generation clientele base rather than to be a guy hoping someone walks through the door willing to sit down in the chair. That is not only inconsistent but it's also awkward. I'm trying to get my clientele where I'm booked out every day of the week. I don't want to be booked only on high-volume days which are traditionally, Friday and Saturday. Only to turn around and be dead Tuesday, Wednesday, and Thursday. I want to be booked solid through the week. From experience, what's worked for me is offering my services for free and networking with complete strangers and offering the craziest deals possible. Services that I know they're not getting from anybody else.

When we first opened Taylor Made One in Johnson City back in 2016, I noticed literally six months to the date after we had opened a Smart Cuts franchise chain opened up across the street that conveniently sat right beside Starbucks. I went and introduced myself immediately. Gave them my business card. "I'm a master barber right across from the McDonalds. I'm not here to compete with you. I just wanted to make myself known in case y'all ever need anything. Here's my contact information. If you need anything don't hesitate to reach out to me."

I didn't bust in the door like, "Yo, y'all stepping on my turf? There's not enough room for two barbershops on this block?" I'm glad that I didn't do that because they lasted literally five months. That's not to say that we ran them out of town or anything. In fact, I think it's more of a community testament of preference. I don't believe that Taylor Made is the end all by any means, but Taylor Made is more than just another grooming option. We've made it our business to connect with the local communities on so many levels and giving back is the essence of our mission. Simply put, the community is what keeps our doors open. So it's not any sort of hindrance to return that same energy. We feel like it's our duty. I'm not certain, but maybe they never attempted to go on campus and give students cut discounted cuts, or even a free cut. Connecting with the students on a personal level and not making it so much of a business transaction. They assumed that because they were beside Starbucks if nothing else they'd get overflow clients from people getting coffee. I'm not saying they had a bad business model, it's just that some customers are looking for more than just the hair off there neck and from around the ears. The chair is a sacred space. If used for more than turning over a dollar, the barber/stylist has the privilege to build with people on a personal level. My neighbors at Smart Cuts were really nice people and not to mention talented, but the only way to make it in business is by having the overall approval of the people. Good People make Good Businesses. It's not so much the other way around being all about the Brand. The brand is the vehicle, but the people are the fuel that runs the engine. Make people the essence of your business, and your business will thrive.

In terms of marketing opportunities, I didn't just go to the local campuses. I've also made myself available to the local ghettos as well. I've cut hair everywhere from the projects to the penthouse. I'm everywhere man. Before I go to work or even when I leave the shop, oftentimes I'm still cutting hair. So, I don't see people like "Smart Cuts or Great Clips" or any other establishment as competition simply because every business has its own unique business model. There's no such thing as perfection in business, but the key is to be consistent with client retention and customer service. I've always tipped my hat to anyone who dares entertain the life of an entrepreneur, also known as the land of uncertainty. The only guarantee in the business, is the cost of doing business.

Whenever a customer patronizes my chair, I'm not solely focused on the potential profit. I'm equally concerned about whatever issues or interests they may have. The Pandemic was obviously something that affected everyone. Covid is something that everybody can relate to. The pandemic was unfortunate but is definitely something that we can all relate to. Personally, I lost three family members last Christmas. There's a great chance that some of my clientele has dealt with loss as a result of the coronavirus. When having a conversation like that, it's easy to find common ground when both the barber and client have suffered similar casualties. When leaving the shop, the client more than likely thinks to themselves "My barber is concerned about my personal well-being as well as my family's well-being. People who he's never even met." I don't know too many barbers who make it a point to connect personally with the public. Unfortunately, a lot of barbers only see the craft as a source of income. Looking at it solely from that perspective kills the true aspect of Community. The community is the most valuable part of any barbershop. So that's what I would accredit to building and retaining clientele is being intentional, impactful, and deliberate with your efforts. If people don't accept your initial invitation, don't sweat it. Don't be afraid of the word "no." Today's no, maybe tomorrow's yes.

Something I've been watching here lately is a Colin Kaepernick Special on Netflix called Black & White. Just listening to his journey and how many "No's" he heard along the way is very motivating. Not only did he have a 4.0 GPA in high school, but he was also a crazy three sport athlete not to mention very credible. Most would think with those types of credentials that he would be a clear candidate for any major division one college in the nation. In fact, his story was the exact opposite, almost every college in the nation said no, all except Nevada University. What if he'd given up because of continuously hearing that same word over and over, NO! He definitely wouldn't have gotten drafted, much less been blessed to play in the biggest game in professional football; The Super Bowl. I feel like I can relate to Kaepernick's journey in regard to being rejected constantly. I heard so many no's, I thought I was in a Destiny's Child song or something. Like dog gone, I'm out here doing everything possible to get established, but it just didn't seem to matter. I kept asking myself, "Why is it not coming together like they said it would? I never took into consideration the concept of a seed, time, and harvest. It doesn't happen when you think it should happen. It happens when it's supposed to happen. It happens when you're ready to receive the harvest. If it had happened back when I wanted it to happen, I would have crashed horribly. I feel like I understand the industry and people a little bit better, and have a better appreciation for life, If I would have started sooner than I did, I would have been an epic failure, epic, epic failure.

I wasn't trained enough. At that point, I hadn't been through nearly enough to fully understand the depth of the business. Not to mention, cutting hair and managing people are nowhere near the same thing. In the same regard, cutting hair and managing a company budget are two completely different things. There are many small variables that go into entrepreneurship. A haircut is a product that all barbers produce, but not all barbers produce quality barbershops. It took all those no's to build up my courage and made me realize, no I don't have the experience but that doesn't disqualify me from the race. I had to become aware of what the position required but also immune to the critics. People will forever cast their insecurities on your life if they've given up hope for their own.

At the end of the day, Barbering is Barbering. The only thing that really separates us is our level of accomplishment. I can overcome any obstacle if I make up my mind and stay focused on the task at hand. I'm no different than any other man, I'm just a man that got tired of being tired. I wasn't born into riches or resources. I am extremely grateful for having those experiences and having those doors slammed in my face. Hearing those no's is what builds not only thick skin and character but is what sets the pace to growing, building, and maintaining an established clientele. Patience and effort will get you there but consistency and determination will keep you in the game.

Moving - Clientele

I came out of barber school in 2010, landed a job in Kingsport, Tennessee at Carew Cuts Barbershop, my first shop. I worked there for seven years until I decided to open my own shop, Taylor Made (1) in 2016. When I left Carew Cuts and left Kingsport, I lost 65-70% of my clientele overnight. Not only did I lose clientele, but my booth rent was $100 a week; $400 per month. My shop rent ended up being $2,000 a month. So, I'm going from an established clientele to very few clients, no manpower to help cut, no assistance with bills, and quadrupling my overhead.

I felt like I was in a Mike Tyson fight, back against the wall getting my head beat in. Those experiences taught me a lot and forced me to buckle down even more. I thought I had a lick on it, but I realized that I'd gotten too comfortable in Kingsport at Carew Cuts because that shop already had a decent clientele with good walk-in traffic. I had even built a regular personal clientele of my own. On average, I just had to sit there, and the folk that didn't want to wait on the owner would just fall right into my chair. I cut them good enough to where some of those individuals started coming to me even more. In a way, I feel like I got complacent with that. What that taught me was that I was not only setting myself up for failure but that it's not a good idea for any barber to rely on walk in traffic from the barbershop for sustainability. I mean think about it, what if nobody walks in? That's no way to ensure a consistent pay rate. As barbers, we have the option of adjusting our pay rate depending on our work ethic. The harder you work and the more you put into the craft, potentially the more profitable he or she can be, I'm just as guilty as many barbers out there, I fell into a pool of complacency. I'm embarrassed to say that it's common in this industry. It becomes so easy to do just enough to get by and still make an average income. Doesn't require a ton of effort, just showing up to the shop and waiting on walk in traffic, still pays the bills. Doesn't leave much extra but definitely can carry the individual from month to month.

What I learned with my transition and "starting over" is that the biggest blessing in my life, has come from the greatest struggles. A lot of barbers go to these shops that have established walk-in traffic and what they don't realize is, if that particular shop closes down so does their career. The shop becomes the blessing instead of the license to cut, being the blessing. Being reliant on the shop puts the barber in a position mentally to depend on "good days/busy days" in order to sustain the barber. The building or regrowing clientele becomes foreign because the barber becomes so used to being spoon fed.

I didn't officially hire my first barber until five months into the business. We didn't get fully staffed until after our first year. So in essence, I cut almost every head in the building, and until we became completely staffed there was very little profit after the overhead was paid in full. The majority of the money that came in was used to keep the doors open. In the previous shop that I worked in, I made decent money because the only overhead I had was booth rent. Not to mention I had a steady clientele that I could depend on. Opening my own barbershop, my baby; Taylor Made One was the greatest challenge of my life. It taught me that I still needed time to fully understand everything about the business. Cutting hair and running a shop is not the same thing. I was in desperate need of barbers, nobody to back me up and help cut the overflow traffic or help supplement the overhead. It almost took me under, I'm not going to lie but looking back on it, man, what a journey! It forced me to grow up, man. It made me more of a complete barber. It made me a man's man because, in my opinion, a real man doesn't cower down to life's challenges.

I was having a conversation with a client that I used to cut at Carew Cuts about business ventures. I'm now cutting him and his son, it's kind of crazy how life works. I love it though. Anyhow, Mr. Jaylen Wells was asking me, "What's a good idea for a new business." I said, "Do a food truck." He replies, "Man, I'm scared of failing." I reply, "Young brother, you have to embrace that. Realize you're going to fail and, by failing, it doesn't mean the business is going to blow up in your face. When you quit, that's when it's over. Failure is essential to the success of any business. It plays a significant part in the process of success. Having to learn that myself, forced me to adapt to all types of pressure."

I would definitely say being forced to start can be a major blessing to any barber along their journey because if you move, not just like me from city to city ... you can go from Tennessee to California, and you're already equipped to form a sufficient clientele. You're bold enough to rebuild what you've lost. If you've already done it, what's to stop you from going to Alaska and doing it again? However, if you've never done it you'll be stuck in this little convenient box because that safe space is what's always provided for you. It's proven to be a consistent source. I would say to any barber, embrace life's challenges and never run from what could potentially propel you towards more. I'm not by any means suggesting that you quit your job and go to another shop or open a shop right out of the gate. What I am saying is don't run from obstacles. Use them as fuel and allow them to elevate you. Realize what it's going to take to get through them but accept them. After all, pressure and inconvenience are key ingredients in building character.

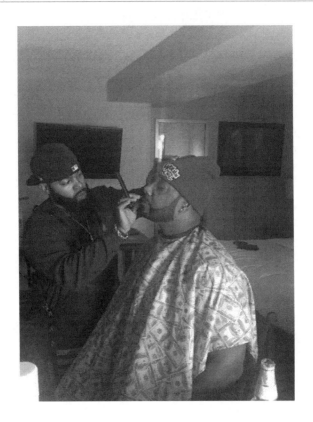

CHAPTER TEN:
OWNING THE SHOP

I own my shop, but I would not consider myself a "business owner" just yet. Mainly because I'm the hardest working barber in my business and on average, business owners don't clock in. They create a structure and a blueprint for the business, and they hold their employees accountable for maintaining a certain level of integrity to keep that structure going. Until I back away from my business and it runs smoothly as I want it to without me being there, I don't feel as if I've earned the title of really considering myself a business owner. I do own my shop, in fact, I own a couple of locations. Please don't mistake owning the business for extensive free time and money. In fact, someone like myself spends more time at work than anywhere else. Let's not forget the business expenses which at times seem endless.

But even outside of that, I don't own either building that my shops sit in, which is another level of ownership. An ideal position in business would be to have full control of the land, building, and business. Having a structure in place and being out of that business with it servicing the community as if you were still there. A structure that doesn't require the owner to clock in and clock out. With enough time invested and restructuring of the business, I hope to be on the way to complete ownership. I'm currently in the process of meeting with a potential real estate investor to begin the purchasing process. I'm at a place in my journey where if I had to, I'd close up shop until the right opportunity came along. I've already left one shop to open this shop. I'll just close this location and put it in another location. In essence, I'll do whatever is required to sustain and grow the brand. In order to grow properly, the sole proprietor must evaluate all business expenses. Deem what's a necessary and unnecessary expense. In my case, the amount of money that I've paid over the last five years proves that I can afford a mortgage for the business. Paying rent money when I could be paying a mortgage and putting the company in an overall better position for future endeavors. At this point in my journey, I'm not making the best use of my capital.

I think ownership is essential but owning your destiny as well as owning your time is more valuable to me than owning "capital". Money's a tool. Money's not even real. They print it and they don't have enough gold to back it. They just keep printing it. I do think it's essential to have a game plan in order to own but a lot of folks, especially in the neighborhood I grew up in, think that putting their name on something essentially means that they're a "boss". That's so far from the truth. That's so, so, so, so far from the truth. Remember, as I mentioned before, real bosses don't punch the clock. So having a title doesn't necessarily free up that individual. In most cases, these so called positions of authority come with more responsibility. The modern-day workforce is a key example of business modification. The average employee is overworked and underpaid. Which keeps everyone in the rat race. Opening your own business doesn't necessarily mean freedom from escaping the rat race. There are so many different levels of slavery nowadays, it's not even funny.

In fact, I feel like personally, they modernized slavery. Instead of specific people of color being in bondage, they just made everybody a freaking slave. A lot of working people don't even realize that their operating within a modernized slave structure. A lot of folks' dreams and ambitions are shackled and chained, and they don't even know it. They're enticed by things like bonuses, promotions, 401ks. All those things are great. I'm not trying to dismantle them whatsoever, but those things, in my opinion, are distractions that keep the individual from really tapping into their true destiny and experiencing their full worth. To me, everyone's definition of ownership should be different. I've given my own, and that's not to say that my views on business owners are the only proven successful way. This is just what I feel is best for my specific journey in business. Rest assured; everyone's journey looks different.

Some folks might look where I'm at and say, "I want what he's acquired and I'm good. If I can just be like Micah Taylor and own a few shops, I have no desire to own the building. I don't want to pay taxes on that property. I want the landlord to deal with the HVAC system. I want the landlord to pay the unexpected expenses on that property. I'll just pay the rent and I'm cool." That might be their peak ideal of ownership and success. It's just not mine. I think you must be in control of the full spectrum, or you're not fully in the driver's seat.

Take Ray Croc for example. He literally took McDonald's from the McDonald brothers and not only made it his own, but he built it worldwide. Initially, he bought into the company as co-owner but eventually bought out the brothers. No longer focusing on the profits from Burger sales but putting more value on owning the restaurant as well as the land on which it sits on. In essence, McDonald's is equally as much of a real estate company as it is a restaurant. With Mr. Crocs' vision, Mickey D's is now top 10 companies in the World.

A great idea with no long-term goals is simply put; a great idea. In order to fully maximize any idea, the visionary must think beyond what he or she sees in the physical. Amazing things can happen when ordinary people take unordinary risks. In the words of Mr. Croc himself, "When I first laid my eyes on McDonald's, I knew I had to have it." Ray not only bought out the brothers, but he also closed down the original location and they never flipped another burger. I'm in no way suggesting that anyone be cut-throat in order to grow in life or in business. I personally feel like

Mr. Crocs' methods were a tad bit devious. However, had he never embraced the challenge, McDonalds could have stayed on the west coast and never grown to the ranks of global franchising. Ray Croc was the definition of Tenacious. He wasn't known for flipping burgers, but he bought land in bulk and that's what allowed him to buy out his partners. So just looking at similar stories like that, the entrepreneur must go deep to the root and see what really makes him or her a "boss". Real leaders push the agenda, not just sit back from a distance cracking the whip. You got to kind of get in the thicket and lead by example.

Even when I am able and blessed to not work as many hours, I will still be very much hands on with the day-to-day operation. I won't ever just expect my barbers to work like I'm doing now 50, 60-hour weeks just to make sure the "customer" is taken care of. No, take care of your family, take care of your kids. If you're married, take care of your spouse. That's your first business. Customer service is and should be the priority but ultimately, the hair grows back. I don't recommend that anyone overexert themselves as I did. It's impossible to cut every head, although I've attempted it before. It's my wish that my barbers understand the importance of great customer service, but it's easy to get burned out in this field. I'd much rather they enjoy the craft and learn a sense of balance along the way. After all, work is work. Family, on the other hand, family is everything.

I want the brand to stand for more than grooming but quality as well. Adding overall value to the consumer's life. I believe our qualities should match destiny. I'm very much concerned with the overall well-being of the crew. Barbers are not machines, they are people. Considering I've been a booth renter longer than a business owner, I try my best to reason with my team. It's important to me that everyone is heard and that their feelings are considered. I ask questions such as, "What do you want out of this job? What's your end goal? Are you interested in empowering people?" I'm all in, rather they want to stay on board with me long-term and help grow the brand or even help them branch out and get their own brand. I'm realizing that this is a bigger part of my calling. I thought it was to be a barber and to be a shop owner, but I'm realizing my job is really meant to mentor and motivate and develop the next generation of leaders, owners, and barbers, or what have you. I was too shallow in my outlook thinking that it was about me and my family, and we'll reap a small benefit of the harvest, but I'm meant to plant a seed, water the seed, and grow fruit. If I can do that successfully and efficiently, I think that's what really makes me a true owner of the brand which I created. A brand that stands for the overall empowerment of people. Something meant to impact far more than the grooming industry.

I can honestly say that a lot of business owners that I know are self-absorbed. They don't think outside themselves. They don't value or consider people. People are literally pawns in their personal chess game. That's one thing that I hate because you don't have to step on another man's neck in order to elevate. We can all eat at the same table. If you and I personally are eating together and your plate's bigger than mine that should motivate me to grind harder so that I can eat more. I shouldn't look at you with animosity and jealousy and think, "Oh, he's eating more than me." I should be blessed to share a meal at the table with you. And while we're eating, I should open my ears and open my heart and learn everything that I can from someone close to me who's conquered the art of More. Don't let jealousy rob you of potential growth. Remain a student for the rest of your life and live to learn. Information changes situations.

As for the good, I know a small handful of good business people. I'll be honest. Again, business as you know, it's a very vicious game, man. Its dog eats dog out here. There's not a lot of love in business and that's where I want to be the exception, in not just barbering but business as a whole. I don't mind if the young ones succeed me and go further than me. That doesn't bother me, not even a little bit. I consider it a blessing because you can only tell a tree if it's bearing fruit. I know a lot of withered up hollow, shallow trees out here, man. The things that I've taken and learned from both the good and bad examples.

Something I really appreciate about the first shop I worked at in Kingsport Tennessee, is the accessibility of the owner, Mr. Richard Jackson. He wasn't closed off, instead, he was an open book of information and he poured into me everything I wanted to know about the trade. The so-called bigger picture. He never saw me as a threat and I'm forever grateful to him for that. He entrusted me wholeheartedly with his business and gave me a key on day one. I personally don't believe in handing out keys to the shop without them being earned, but he knew within a couple of weeks of working with me, this is a young man who not only has what it takes to be a barber but is completely dedicated to something that's not even his own. That's definitely a quality that I wish to embody, that sense of community. The power of us, as my grand use to say, "Strength In Numbers". Not seeing your neighbor as a threat but instead as a potential resource. Someone to build with.

Owning my own shop has taught me that there are truly no ceilings. There are not a lot of business owners or owners of any regard in my family. It's not necessarily a bad thing, but being an entrepreneur has taught me, that if I can leave a seven to eight year established clientele that won't follow me and rebuild on the second level of a two-story building with no handicapped accessibility what else can we do? Six years in and we've not only figured out how to rebuild from scratch but also during a global pandemic. Something no one was prepared to deal with. We started renovations on TMII Pre-Covid. Forced to pull the trigger on a grand opening after a global lockdown. Talk about being forced to make some quick adjustments. Especially when there's a stack of bills due and no money coming in due to being deemed "Nonessential" by the government. As I mentioned before, the business world is a tough and rather harsh reality. There are two basic options in business, sink or swim.

I'm now wanting Taylor Made to be a brand. Not Taylor Made

barbershop, but the Taylor Made man. Since our grand opening, we've released a small line of apparel. Our biggest product is our in-house beard butter made by hand. We cut quite a few clients with beards, so it's rather refreshing to send them home with a product that can not only maintain the overall health of their beard but keeps it smelling fresh and clean as well. I'm starting to think, my product only sells to men with beards. Most men that come to my shop don't even have beards. So, I've created a product that I can't even sell to the masses. Now I have a product that I can only sell to men with beards and or barbers in the community. This forced me to think more outside the box. It's helped me see the brand in its entirety.

How can I create something that's non-barber related, that's non-gender biased, something that a woman would want to wear? Everyone should want to be Taylor Made. Everyone's dreams and lifestyle should be literally Taylor Made. You customize your dreams, your living and your home life. If you want to vacate, you should Tailor your journey. You should be intentional with that. So, opening the business has taught me I should set a plan in motion and do whatever the heck it takes to see it through. Be intentional about everything I do and work hard for results. That's the only true way to guarantee real positive results in the world of business.

CONCLUSION

If you focus enough on what's going on around you in life, everybody has their struggles and their battles. If you focus enough on the noise outside of your own heart, you'll be immediately defeated and discouraged. It will really, really rob you of any potential traction. You have to get traction to get to your destination. You got to build up traction. If you turn on the news, you turn on social media, even friends... I mentioned earlier that my family grew up in a very, very poverty-stricken area. To them, if the food stamp card is coming on time and we get food in the fridge, and the bills are paid, we're good. That is so wack to me.

It bothers me that a lot of my family has completely just settled and kind of thrown the God-given abilities and potentials to the wayside because it's going to take more than they're willing to put in. It's going to take all the intestinal fortitude. It's going to take sleepless nights, long, long, long hours, and days. It's going to drain you and you're going to feel like a lot of the times that you're not getting anywhere, you're not making any traction, but you have to listen to the beat of your own heart and follow the beat of your own drum. And you got to motivate yourself.

I also mentioned in the previous chapters that I get up at five o'clock every morning. I work out, not to be Mr. Muscle mania, but it's so quiet. On my drive to the gym, isn't nobody on the road. Everybody's knocked out. So, I talk to myself. It sounds crazy, but when I'm in my car and its 5:00 AM, I turn the radio down. Even freezing cold outside right now, I roll the windows down. I'll talk to the universe. I'll put my plans out in the universe and I started encouraging myself. "All right, Micah, we are going to do X, Y, Z. All right, by this time next year, it's going to look like X, Y, Z."

I'm intentional with my plans and I'm intentional with encouraging myself. Even when I get to the gym and I get my headphones and my Beats on, I get my music crank so loud. I'm singing Nas to the next man beside me. He looks like this man has lost his freaking mind. Nas new album is called King's Disease. I feel like I can relate to a lot of the content this brother is spitting. So as I'm throwing my bench press, I'm doing my curls and whatever I'm doing, I'm literally reciting lyrics out loud to the point where they look at me like I'm crazy.

Stay away from that dude. He's a little off his rocker. I want you to think that. I want you far away from me because you're probably here trying to get cute for some kind of trip you're going on. When the trips are over, you go back to dad bod and beer gut, cholesterol, and hypertension which I'm trying to beat. I'm not here for that, man. I got a hellacious day in front of me. As soon as I get out of this gym and get out of my shower, the pressure is all the way on. If I condition my mind enough, I don't care what you throw at me. I hit back so hard that you thought you were in a battle with Tyson, man, literally. So, I bump my Nas. I bump my TD Jakes.

Jake's has a story that like my own comes from humble beginnings out of the hills of West Virginia. He started out with a congregation of just 50 people, but folk Covet his current position. They Covet his current congregation. They covered his millions. They covered his several thousand congregational ministries. You don't want that man's problems. You don't want his debt, you don't want his Journey nor his challenges! You can't even be faithful to the little bit, but you want his success? So, it's a process on every level. Most folks are not willing to go through the process. You have to go through the process and everybody's process is different. Mine just so happened to be barbering in my area, and in my craft, my industry, I've done barbering probably on a level that's never been done. Not because I'm great, not because I'm Micah. I made up my mind then, this is what we are doing.

More importantly, the buck stops here. It's so crazy. I got my son thinking that he can literally jump off a building and fly. My son doesn't believe in limits. My son told me something crazy. Three weeks ago, I was praying for him. I put some oil on him, and was just talking to him and encouraging him and building him up like I usually do. I said, "Man, stay away from people. When you're not going to class or practice, kind of stay to yourself. COVID is out here. COVID is real and it's taking folk out." He's like, ``Pop, I can't get COVID." I said, "Huh?" He said, "You prayed for me." He said, "God, isn't deaf." He said, "I'm covered, man, and so are you, so is mom." He's like, "I'm on a team that 80% has contracted COVID and I haven't yet. My roommate, I transported him in my car. I didn't tell you because I knew you'd be mad. I took him in my car to the hospital to make sure he was going to be right, and I still didn't contract it. He's breathing all over my car. I didn't catch it."

He's like, "I'm covered by the grace of God." I've never heard him speak so boldly before about his faith. I have never heard him be so radical. Not only does he believe it, but he still has yet to contract it. I think more or less, it starts because he showed God that I trust you. I trust you with my whole heart, but I'm trying to, I guess, reaffirm to him, "You can trust God, but you've got to be smart, son. You can't just open yourself up to the attacks of the enemy because that's where he creeps in and does most of his damage."

But I say it to say, just looking at his life, he embraces the challenges and he embraces the obstacles. He kind of lives like he's made out of Teflon. I think it's because I don't complain to him. I don't let him see me sweat. I don't let him see the depth of the struggle. He reaps the benefit from the journey, not the hardship. So hopefully, my grandkids, man, will kind of be on some fresh prince of Bel Air status, hopefully. I hope so. Hopefully, they're just little miniature optimistic and positive individuals walking around here and my prayer is that we don't have to talk about this poverty crap no more, man. That's my plan because I feel like we all are equipped and we all have gifts and we all have a purpose. You don't just creep up into this thing by chance.

It isn't that two people got together and got intimate and you popped out. If anything, you won the race of how many millions of sperm. You all started the line, on your mark, got set, and Oliver T Reed won the race. He broke the ribbon, man. That's how he came up with this thing. So, you came into this thing as a champion, as a winner. So I would just say in conclusion to block out the noise, create your own noise, create your own madness. Pull from that madness. If there's pain that's been occurring or reoccurring in your life, don't be overtaken by it. Pull from it. Pull from it, man. Grow from it, learn from it, and kill it. Don't let that be somebody else's pain. My lineage, it's like we're passing the buck.

It's almost like, I'm hurting so you're going to hurt. I never met my grandfather. I have no clue what that man looks like. I know he caused my father pure immortal hell and, because of that, my relationship with my dad was strenuous. That's not going to be my son's story, man. My son has absolutely nothing to do with what took places with previous generations. So just kind of killing that negative energy, but more so pulling from it instead of letting it be the driving force. I don't believe in exceptional people. I believe in exceptional grind, exceptional focus, exceptional hustle, and exceptional planning.

I don't think nobody's great. Michael Jordan didn't win six because he's Michael Jordan. He worked his butt off, man. Because of that Kobe Bryant patented his game. He won five. Because of that, LeBron patented his game and he's won three or four, whatever the case might be. You get my point, man. People are motivated by great successors and success stories. They pull from that stuff.

It's so easy to do nothing, but society was created that way. They want you to do nothing. They want the wealthy to be that small percentage because, if everyone was wealthy, that means everyone has options. And not just options, they have influence. If everybody had wealth and options and influence, I believe wholeheartedly we could bust this thing wide open. Especially African Americans, we could be the ones with acres and acres of land. Forget businesses, let's own land. Instead of going to Disney World, let's go to some deserted island where nobody's at, some private island that we own and stay as long as we want. Serious options, not just taking a few day vacation, but we could literally write our own story, whatever that looks like for us.

That starts with intentional focus, and I just feel like as people, we've been dealt a couple of wild cards and a couple of jokers. I feel like we've just taken the bait. Even this year marks 100 years of a Tulsa, Oklahoma Massacre. The first bombing on American soil. They bombed us, man. They bombed our potential. But if we could do that in 1921, my God, what can we do in 2022? But it starts with unity. It starts with faith, with love. I shouldn't be the slightest bit inferior to you. If you're more than me and you've done more in your life than I have, I should be a student and I should be open and willing to learn and pull from and grow with you. But I feel like, as blacks, we've been trained so much through the Willy Lynch syndrome and system to be each other's competition instead of each other's help.

I feel like the Jews and the Spanish have mastered the art of community and we have yet to figure out what is necessary to get past these years of just dysfunction, poverty, and poison. It's not about money. It's not about authority or position. It's about just living life like you're supposed to as a lot of other folks do. I grew up playing ball with a lot of kids who come from money, I spent a few weekends with them. We went to their grandparents' lake house, riding jet skis. I pulled up in the Yukon and never saw any mess like that. Y'all out here living life to the fullest. So, we're at the lake chilling and grilling ribeye steaks, filets, ribs and whatever we want because money isn't a thing to them.

They're not going into debt to "live life" or "turn up." They're pulling from their source to live life on their own terms. I've seen it too many times as a young man. My reality is not real. Even though I'm stuck in this mess right now where I'm living and what I'm dealing with, what I'm forced to deal with right now, it's not reality. It's a reality someone else has accepted, and I'm here now. It is not how the story ends. So just again, create your own destiny, form your own plan. Believe in yourself because nobody else ever will. Feed your brain constantly with positive, encouraging, and motivating material. That's different for different people.

I'm a lover of Eric Thomas. I think his story is incredible. ET. The hip hop preacher. He preaches to me every morning. When I hear his story and I hear his content, I can run through a wall. So just feed yourself something that's going to literally fuel you instead of pulling the creativity and potential out of you.

To Barber's in School

Don't quit. Stay focused. In your downtime, get rest. A lot of barbers, because we make cash on hand daily, we don't get a paycheck. We get paid daily cash. Don't waste that money or that time. If you are spending time with other barbers, it should be barbers who have the same plans and the same drive as you do. Be very, very, very intentional with who you allow in your space. I thought for the longest time that it was an arrogant statement, but it's not. My time is valuable. My time is more valuable than my money. I can't get it back. If I got $100 in my wallet right now and I lose it, no harm, no foul. I can get it back. If I lose an hour of my day, that's an hour of my life that is never going to return.

So just be focused out the gate, run with like-minded individuals. Run with a pack of lions. Don't just buddy up with anybody just for company's sake. Don't get so caught up in the social media thing of clout chasing. All that stuff is a facade anyway. Just being intentional. Shop ownership is not for everybody. Understand that from the jump. I think a lot of students crave ownership simply to have respect from their peers. I'm already a licensed instructor. When I teach at the academy, nine out of 10 students tell me their dream one day is to open a shop one day.

The problem with that is everybody's not meant to be an owner. Somebody got to be a worker. That doesn't make you less of a person or a barber. Just know your place. Know that if you do own a shop, they might overtake you and take you out. So just realizing your place in this whole thing, and being intentional.

A Sanctuary

I think some things that are needed are looking at what's been done in our industry in years past and doing the exact opposite. That's what I did. I'm not some success story. I'm just somebody who was a student of the game and paid attention to what wasn't being done and did the exact opposite. I'm really big on community. I think something that will help kill that stigma is thinking outside the haircut and the money and building relationships, especially with the babies. Yeah. I'm 40 years old, but I am 10-year-old. I'm in church this morning and I had a young man make his mom stop her car in the line coming into the church because he was walking across the parking lot. I hear him as the window rolls down, "Mom, that's Micah, that's Micah." Like I'm freaking Michael Jordan or something. I am nobody. But to that young man, I'm somebody. I'm somebody.

It is beautiful to me to see that because he sees that a barber is influential. A barber is making a difference. I've been having him in my shop for a few months now just sweeping up. I pay him some money, but I'm teaching him a work ethic. I'm teaching him that somebody outside of his mom and his dad and his grandparents loves him, and care about him. Got great plans for him, want to see him succeed. So I think something that'll really help kill that stigma is thinking outside youexcuse myrself, and being selfless. A lot of barbers are selfish. If you make an appointment with them, they might be on time, or they might not. They might take a break on you. They might cut your hair the way you want it if they feel good. They might not. That's wack.

You sign up to be an advocate of the community, a servant of the community. Until we can get those things down pat, I don't think it'll ever change because my industry is not respected. It's because of the players that play the game. It's not because of the industry itself. The industry is one of the oldest professions in this world. That's not an opinion. That's a fact. It dates back to Roman and ancient Egypt times. The emperors and the pharaohs and the Kings and Queens had personal stylists and barbers. That's a fact. So how are we here in 2021 and we're on the low end of the totem pole as far as our respect? It's because somewhere along the line, folk again started getting that cash on hand daily, started to think they were more than what they are, never had a plan, and started disrespecting people.

You have to respect people, even if somebody disrespects you. I've had folk cuss at me in my shop. I'm not going to cuss back at you. I'm not going to stoop to your level. I'm up here. I'm not better than you, but I'm in the clouds. I got up at 5:00 to make sure that, when I get in my cloud, isn't nobody will come in this cloud without my permission. So when you cuss at me, I'm going to counteract with love. I'm going to ask you, can I pray with you? But first, find out what the root of the problem is. "What's troubling you today, man? That's unlike you. What's that about?" If you ask questions, if you have active listening skills, you'll get to the root of a lot of crap real quick.

But most barbers don't, excuse my French, don't give a damn. So until we can change that, the stigma will never change. Unfortunately, I hate to say we have a long way to go. I don't see it changing anytime soon, because most folks are so materialistic driven. It's not even funny. Gucci belts and Louis Vuitton wallets and Jordans, all this stuff's going to burn up one day. There's no value and it can't get you to any destination. But love, genuine, genuine, no strings attached love, that doesn't exist in my industry. So I'm going to be the embodiment of that and Taylor Made the brand, not the barber shop, is going to be a catalyst for that.

It's Neither Black Nor White Heaven

I think another thing that holds back our industry is culture. I know you can relate to what I'm about to say. The few times I got my hair cut in Virginia Beach as a kid, I went to a shop that you would never see a white person walk into. Across town in white Barbershops, all their customers looked just like them. And across the street, Hispanic guys were cutting. All the customers like them. So, we can all get in one room, have open conversation with no feelings attached. I've seen it work time and time again. What I like about my shop is it's very, very multicultural from the staff first. I don't hire all Black people. I got Hispanic, I got White, I got Mixed, I got Black, I got whoever. But because of that and the way I go about setting up my business, I draw a multicultural crowd.

What I love to see is open dialogue with a multicultural group of clients waiting in the lounge area. When we first opened for business, we had a tiny waiting area that almost felt claustrophobic. A year into business, I bought out a suite beside me and turned it into a comfortable area to relax without feeling packed in. So, when you're a young black college student and an old white farmer walks in, and he parks right beside you, I can feel tension so thick I can cut it with a butter knife. But when I get real, real quiet, I hear conversations in that room that probably would've never happened anywhere else had those two not come to the barbershop. That's dope to me, man, because this is a multicultural world. If we all are so fortunate enough and blessed to make it to heaven, everybody's going to be there.

It isn't going to be a black heaven. It isn't going to be a white heaven. It's going to be everybody. So I'm personally tired of seeing segregation in the industry. Everybody needs a haircut and the shop should be for everybody. That should be the shop. Barbers should be fully equipped to cut any culture, and any culture should feel comfortable coming into a black-owned shop if you're not a black man or vice versa. I think those things, along with what I mentioned earlier, are what's really, really, really going to blow this thing out of the water because we all came from one man, and nobody's the exception. Nobody's better than others.

I feel like black people have been through more hell than other people, but that doesn't give us a pass to hang our feelings up on somebody else or snap at a white man because he walks in or get jealous of the Hispanic man because he's figured out the community and we haven't. I feel like we all have a place in this thing. I feel like the barbershop is a place unlike Walmart or the Mall. We all pass by other cultures in shopping centers. But in the barbershop, you're forced to sit down, wait your turn and strike up some kind of dialogue and have some kind of conversation. If you are intentional and open your ears, you just might learn something, because we can all learn from each other.

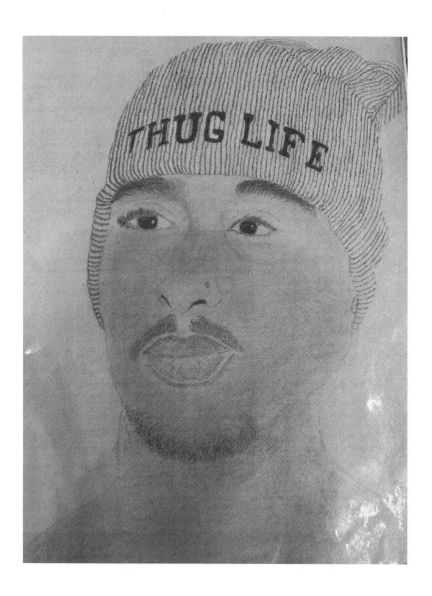

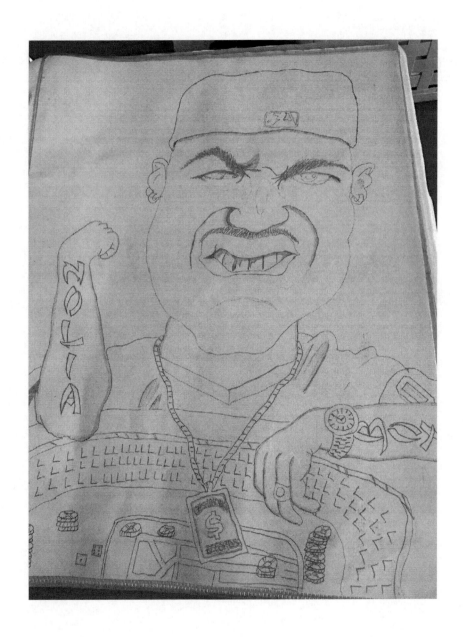

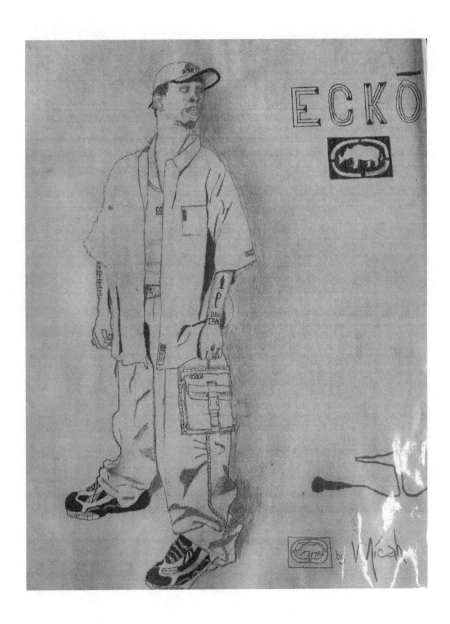

353f4f69-8df2-499c-a35e-469544fcbfbcR02